THE BACKYARD CHICKEN FIGHT

How Keeping Chickens
in Your Yard is Ruffling Feathers
Across the Nation
– AND –
A Beginner's Guide to Hen Keeping

GRETCHEN ANDERSON

with expert chicken advice from Zamzows' Mike Stanton

To Rick!

Happy hen keeping!

Gretchen A

Mill Park Publishing
Eagle, Idaho

Text copyright © 2011 by the author

Images used by permission

Book cover and design by Barbara C. Morris | B. graphic

Back cover and author's portrait by Tyler D. Cazier | Cazier Portraits

Edited by Tanya Eckert and Buster Minshew

ISBN 978-0-9728225-5-8

Printed in USA
Mill Park Publishing
Eagle, Idaho 83616

www.millparkpublishing.com

THE BACKYARD CHICKEN FIGHT

Q: Which Came First?
A: The Introduction.

"Why do you want lame hens?" my husband asked with a wry smile.

"Honey, I said 'laying hens.'"

There was a long pause after that response, and then he said, "I'm pretty certain lame hens won't give you eggs."

Argh! How frustrating.

I've wanted laying hens for years. As a child, my brother and I had 22 hens and one rooster. To earn spending money, we would peddle our bicycles around the neighborhood selling eggs to anyone who would buy them. The old German grandma, who was a fabulous baker, was our best customer.

Finally, after reading an article from a hoity-toity East Coast magazine about the growing trend of urban poultry keeping, I hatched a brilliant idea. I could get some laying hens, team up with one of the area's leading authorities on chickens and write a guide to keeping backyard hens — all the while, I'd chronicle the numerous stories of people fighting to keep chickens in their own backyards. There is no shortage of stories from across the country. From northern Massachusetts to Southern California and all points in between, Americans want to keep chickens.

The backyard chicken movement has been fueled by the growing emphasis on eating fresh and local. People want to know from where their food comes. As a result, more and more Americans are gardening in whatever space they have and they are raising chickens, effectively reducing their carbon footprint. Chickens provide a bounty of eggs, abundant organic fertilizer and natural pest control. They also provide hours of entertainment, companionship and pleasure.

More than 500-million eggs were recalled.

I began research on this book months before the massive, nationwide recall of some 500-million eggs. To date, this is the largest recall of eggs on record. More than 2,000 consumers were sickened by the Salmonella outbreak that occurred in Iowa, where the U.S. Food and Drug Administration inspected the farms and found evidence of poor health standards. The recall extended to Arkansas, California, Illinois, Indiana, Iowa, Kansas, Minnesota, Missouri, Nebraska, North Dakota, Ohio, South Dakota, Texas, and Wisconsin. Those supporting the efforts to keep small, manageable flocks in their backyards felt this huge recall lent great legitimacy to their argument.

Please enjoy the short stories from around the country of the fights to keep feathered friends in the backyard. You don't need to read this little book from start to finish. Use this book as a reference guide for your own little brood and skip around to the stories — they're inspiring!

Acknowledgments

Special thanks to my chicken guru, Mike Stanton of Zamzows. Additional thanks to Mike's bosses, Randy Corn and Darin Eisenbarth for the use of the Zamzows break room and Mike's time with me on Friday mornings. Thanks for the help I received from Jan Davis, Ashlynn Thompson and Art Gregory. I offer gratitude to my editors, Tanya Eckert and Buster Minshew — the two best pair of eyes I know. Props to my designer and former high school classmate, Barbara C. Morris of B. graphic. You were the best designer back then — and you still are! Thank you to my publisher, Mill Park Publishing. And, thanks to my family, especially to Maggie who accompanied me on many "chicken research" outings and wrote the chapter on "4-H: You and Your Chicken."

CHAPTER 1

For the Love
of the Chicken

Just as soon as I told friends about my "chicken project," the stories came my way. Many of them are funny. Some are sad and others just darn inspiring. Here is a small collection of the tales.

This story is personal and came to me twice, once from my son and then from a good friend.

Rogue Rooster Adopts City Corner

Our son came home from canvassing our downtown area to promote his high school theatrical production. I asked him how it went, he told me, "Great!" Then he regaled me with a story about a rooster strutting through the middle of town. I asked him where, he said, "Like … the old State Street area." Mind you, this is coming from a 14-year-old boy who gets side-tracked when he goes out to the garage to fetch a gallon of milk. The point is, he came home pretty excited to tell me about this rooster because he knows I have a penchant for poultry. I shrugged it off thinking he had seen a wayward rooster that belonged to someone and it wasn't that big of a deal.

Karen Sassadeck and Red.

It wasn't until my friend Mary told me the same thing that my curiosity piqued. "A rooster has adopted a busy corner in town and when a lady complained to the cops that he wouldn't let her pass by, they told her to cross the road! Ha, the chicken made the lady cross the road!"

Turns out, this was no ordinary rooster. He does indeed patrol the southwest corner of State Street and Kestrel in Eagle, Idaho, where chiropractor Larry Sassadeck has his clinic. He's protecting his adopted family at the clinic — including all the patients who visit.

The office manager and Larry's better half, Karen Sassadeck, has named him "Red." He's a golden Campine and the nicest rooster I've ever encountered. All the stories I've heard, and my experience as a kid taught me to stay away from roosters. Not so with this guy. He is charming and obviously trusts Karen. She'll call out to him in her sweetest "cock-a-doodle-doo." He answers back and runs to her from out of the bushes.

Red took up residency in the heat of the summer, but neighbors report spotting him as early as May. He roosts at night in one of the trees near the clinic. During the day he eats food that Karen provides and he greets people who arrive for their appointments. According to Karen he has never become cross with a patient — but for one woman who was adorned with a big red hat and big sunglasses. "He got his hackles up and became very defensive," Karen recalls. He has protected the corner from joggers, ne'er-do-wells and unleashed dogs. And, as Karen tells it, he will do this by going at the target, hackles up, feet-first!

Still, Red is comfortable around humans, so much so that Karen can hold him and massage his comb and wattles. At the Sassadeck clinic, you can get acupuncture and massage — but I don't think they ever thought they would massage wattles.

—G.A.

Chicken Have Feelings Too

"Two of our hens were brooding fertile eggs together. Each day the ladies would take turns away from their nest and when they were there together on their nest box they would have a wing draped over the other one's back the entire time they sat together. My birds seem to know their names, know their routine (like what 'bedtime' means), and appear to recognize people with whom they are familiar. I can call out from the house with an individual bird's name and a threatening tone when they are being naughty, and that bird will freeze in her tracks and cease the behavior. They really are amazing, charismatic beings, which is why I believe poultry keeping is so outrageously popular."

—*Michelle Koeppe, Portland, Oregon*

Yes, You Can Walk Your Chicken

"When my brother was in high school, one year his girlfriend gave him two baby chickens as an Easter present. I remember my mom wanted to get rid of them, but I begged her to let me keep them. I was about 12 years old at the time.

I named them Spiro and Millhouse (yes we were in that era). We lived in suburban Salt Lake City, Utah, at the time. On Yalecrest Avenue, it didn't get any more typical of a SLC neighborhood than that. I built the chickens a little pen in our backyard. My sister, Julie was so mad at me because as the chickens got older, they started crowing really early every morning. The neighbors complained too. But I loved my little chickens and defended their crowing. I thought that perhaps they needed a little exercise, so I crocheted leashes for them. I would take them for walks around the block with their crochet leashes around their ankles. Life was great. I was so excited to have my dad teach me how to hypnotize a chicken (an art his father taught him). Wow, what more could a chicken lover want? Then to my dismay, one day the neighbor's cat broke into our backyard and ate my chickens. I was so sad. The next summer I went on to get banty show chickens — but Salt Lake suburbia was not ready for my progressive behavior, and more neighborhood cats came and ate them too. I hate to say it, but I finally gave up my dreams of being a chicken farmer on Yalecrest Avenue."

—*Georgia Hayes, Park City, Utah*

As Friendly as the Other Critters — But Not as Obedient

"As a school science project, we helped raise two Buff Orpington pullets, first in the house in a laundry basket, then in the backyard. Because the chickens were used to being handled, they thought they were 'people' and enjoyed being around people. They would stand on the deck and peck on the French door, trying to get into the house. The funniest situation occurred when my daughter invited one of her former college professors, who was in town for a few days, to come for dinner. After dinner we sat in the backyard in lawn chairs. The chair the professor sat in was made of webbing with an open space between the seat and the back. The pants he was wearing had buttons on the two back pockets. The chickens came up behind him and kept pecking him on the rear as they tried to pull off the buttons. My daughter was embarrassed, but how do you tell a chicken to stop? They don't obey like a dog or even a cat. The professor said it was the first time he had been 'attacked' by a chicken. He found the humor in the situation, as we all did."

—*Glenna Tooman,* Boise, Idaho

Chickens as a Way of Life

"My husband and I own five pet chickens in a suburb of Los Angeles. I moved here from New York City, so you can imagine after 20 years in the urban jungle how funny it is to now be so well versed in chicken raising. I completely understand how these crazy little creatures worm their way into a person's life and heart. Before raising them, chickens were simply bland breasts and legs in plastic wrap in the market. Now I can distinguish what each of their sounds mean, who wants what, who's whining and who's just laid an egg. We've had to deal with all sorts of chicken drama, including chicken-on-chicken violence, rushing a brutally attacked teenage hen into chicken micro-surgery (complete with a little beak-shaped gas mask), a chicken vet named Dr. Tyson (we hoped this wasn't a bad omen), chicken boot camp for a misbehaving flock member, and ultimately finding a chicken rescue facility for our Rhode Island Red, Ginger (alas, she went crazy). We went from rank beginners to experts!

I completely understand why people raise chickens and why it's gaining in popularity. They provide comfort and companionship by keeping me company when my husband travels, often sitting on the porch outside my home office while I work. They also provide unending amusement. There are few things funnier than seeing a bunch of birds that are built like sumo-wrestlers running at full tilt, one after another, flapping furiously, when the first one spies a bug and stops short. The pile-up of beaks and bulbous bodies is hilarious and ridiculous! After a hard day of work, I come home and they race toward me from all corners of the yard to greet me with what I like to think is love, but is really just the search for grapes. Each girl is different. When you get to know animals at this level, it's hard not to become obsessed. Even if it's a chicken. On a daily basis they provide simple pleasures for me and as I get older this becomes more and more of a priority. More and more people are realizing this. In this crazy world of unending distractions and complications, they offer a sweetness and simplicity few other things do.

While I like to think that I'm sophisticated, I admit that I now subscribe to *Backyard Poultry Magazine* and participate in the online forums. I've become much more aware of where my food comes from. There's nothing quite like a fresh egg that is still warm from being laid moments ago. The brilliant orange yolk, the hard shell and unequalled taste require you to examine and be connected to your food source. This concept was something I had never thought of before. Now, I do, and not because it's trendy. It's just real."

—Andie Cohen-Healy, Altadena, California

They Really Do "Come Home to Roost"

"We have a flock of about 30 chickens. One particular winter day, it was cold, snowy and miserable, and the girls had been locked in the coop for a long while. When the kids opened the door to check on their water, one of the hens escaped out into the cold and snow, and vanished. Oh well, we thought, that's the end of her. The snow and bitter cold went on for many days, and then one day, she just wandered up to the door of the hen house as we went to gather eggs. Where she had been we assume there was no food, all the water sources were hard frozen, and there was nowhere for her to get shelter from the snowstorms. Yet she seemed fine. We named her 'Lazarus'."

—Martin Focazio, Conshohocken, Pennsylvania

Show & Tell

"When I was a child we had a hen named 'Freckles'. She was a black and white speckled bantam. She would peck on the door when she wanted in. My mom had a box with some straw in it placed between the washer and dryer in the utility room. Freckles would come in, get in her box and lay her egg, then peck on the door to go back out. She did this every day until she had about eight eggs and then she sat on those eggs until they hatched into fluffy yellow chicks. As children in grade school, we would take Freckles and her babies to school for 'show and tell'. This was a yearly ritual for many years.

Now as an adult, I still raise chickens. They are just as much a pet as dogs or cats. Mine come to greet me every time I go to their pen. They want to be held and cuddled and if I don't pick them up when they want me to, they let me know about it. They will pull on my pants leg or if I'm wearing shorts they will jump up and grab the leg of my shorts. They love to sit on my lap and are so jealous they will try to knock each other off for the prized spot."

—Liz Modrell, Sperry, Iowa

Call Her Eighty-Nine

"My husband raises chickens, so we have several dozen around all the time. Last fall, one of our hens became attached to me. Every time I went to feed and change the chicken's water, this particular hen would come up to me. She would sit next to me when I changed the water and let me pet her. She would also cackle at me when she saw me, as if she was talking to me. Over the course of a month, I noticed she was becoming detached from the other chickens. She would stand alone in the chicken yard, or stay in the coop with her face to the wall as if she was hiding from the other chickens. The others had also started to pick on her, so she was starting to look beat up. The only time she showed any energy was when I came into the yard or coop to feed.

My husband and I decided to move her into a hutch by herself to monitor her, which has led to her becoming our pet chicken. She is tagged with the number 89, so 89 has become her name. She responds to me when I talk to her and twice a day I take her out of her hutch for a walk (I carry her) and for play time. She has a separate covered outdoor area where she can roam and hunt for bugs without having to interface with any other chickens. She loves the attention and enjoys being a pet. She likes to be patted on her chest and back and sometimes likes to be scratched near the top of her head. She has become accustomed to a routine and knows exactly what to do when I open the door to her hutch. She will turn her body a certain way that makes it easy for me to pick her up and take her out. She knows that when we open the hutch door in the morning that she gets some one-on-one time with me, a good petting, and a walk to her outdoor recreation area. I never thought I would become attached to a chicken, but this one has captured my heart."

—*Christine Tanzillo, Canton, Texas*

Swanky Abode

"We recently added chickens to our household. Our city, Ypsilanti, Michigan, allowed an ordinance earlier this year for four egg-laying chickens, but no roosters. My husband was thrilled and rushed out to build a swanky chicken coop with materials from other home improvement projects around our house.

One of my friends remarked, 'French doors? I don't have such nice doors! That coop is nicer than my condo!'"

—*Julie Collins, Ypsilanti, Michigan*

A True Urban Chicken

"I work from a home office and live in the heart of Los Angeles with my neighborhood right in the middle of four main, well-trafficked streets. About three-and-a-half years ago, over the din of cars, I heard a noise coming from below my second story window that I hadn't heard before. I looked out, and there in the small front yard of my corner apartment was something I never expected to see.

There was a chicken calmly walking around the yard pecking at the grass. Even in the very urban Los Angeles environment we do have our share of wild animals including coyotes, raccoons and opossums, but seeing a roaming chicken was like seeing snow on the streets. It just doesn't happen. My first thought was that someone's pet chicken got out, and being the animal do-gooder I am, I went down to see if I could possibly capture her and keep her safe while I put up some signs in the neighborhood. I learned pretty quickly that a chicken that doesn't want to get caught can be pretty quick, and because I was afraid it would run out into the street, I decided it would be best to try to feed her and maybe the owner would come by.

I grabbed what I thought would be the most appropriate chicken food, some corn I had in the freezer that I heated and then cooled, and went back down to the yard where she seemed to be oblivious to the cars slowing, stopping and pointing. I laid the corn out and moved away a bit. After a few tentative moves toward it, she finally took a taste. And that was the start of a beautiful friendship.

For the next three years, between 3:00 and 3:30 p.m., like clockwork, I would look out my window and see her across the street waiting. I would walk outside with her food (the frozen corn was a staple of her diet), and as soon as she'd see me she'd meander across the street. Thankfully, there were stop signs on the four corners and she learned how to time her move. My heart would still skip a beat when she'd take her step off the sidewalk and confidently cross over like she owned the neighborhood. And every day I would see the looks on amazed drivers faces. The cell phone cameras would come out and invariably there would be finger pointing and big smiles.

Before too long, she felt safe enough with me to eat out of my hand, and eventually she let me hold and pet her. I wasn't allowed to have animals in the apartment I had moved to, so these 10 or 15 minutes a day we'd spend together became very important to me. Some of the more enjoyable times were when the kids from the neighborhood stopped by. Like most kids, their first reaction would be to try and catch the chicken. I explained how we didn't want to scare her into the street and then share a few 'fast chicken facts' I'd learned. It was sort of like my little version of a school field trip. I'd ask the kids to give the chicken a name and over the years she must have been known by thirty different names and had hundreds of photos taken of her. I never gave her a name. To me, she was 'sweetheart' or 'baby' or 'goofball'.

After she was done eating we'd spend a little time hanging out and then she'd cross back over to the other side of the street. There was a large tree on the corner with low-hanging branches and she'd walk around and around the base before flapping her wings like crazy, 'jump' up to the first branch and head up farther into the tree. My best guess is that she would wait until dark, jump down and head to wherever she slept for the night. I never figured out where that was, but she was always in her spot the next day, and every day for three years, except when it rained … but how often does that happen in Los Angeles?

And then one day, as mysteriously as she arrived, she just as mysteriously didn't. She just didn't come by. Every day for a couple of weeks I would set her food out in the hopes she would come back. And as strange as it may be, I actually went through a little grieving process like a pet had passed away. I don't know if someone captured her, she was hit by a car or just died in her sleep from old age, which is the explanation that I went with.

That chicken not only brought a lot of joy to me, but to literally hundreds, if not thousands of urban dwellers. She was a wonderful reminder that we're all in this together. And you know what? I haven't eaten chicken in three-and-a-half years."

—T. Fraser, Los Angeles, California

HENceforth: Predators Beware

"It was embarrassing, but also one of my proudest moments. I was in the shower when I heard a terrible commotion outside. The flock of free-range chickens (the Ladies) were screeching. Without thought that I had nothing on, my hair was soapy, and my feet were bare, I dashed out of the house. I found a full-sized hawk on my favorite chicken, Edith, under a bush. The hawk was desperately trying to lift this large Brahma chicken into the air. Edith was giving it her all. I rushed toward them ready to kick the hawk off my favorite hen. Instead, it took one look at my crazed eyes and 'flapping wings' and knew I was no mother hen to mess with. It flew off and Edith was once again safe.

I live in rural Arkansas, on 13 acres — with no neighbors. There was no danger of being seen, other than by the electric meter reader coming up the drive."

—Jacqueline Wolven, Eureka Springs, Arkansas

Mistaken Identity

"My mother thought her chickens had 'flown the coop.' She and a friend chased a flock of very confused hens through town with salmon fishing nets. She returned home, wet and muddy, only to learn they weren't her chickens. She'd netted the wrong birds. While she would have liked to whip up some tasty fried chicken with them...her friend told her she should 'eat crow' instead."

—Cynthia Briggs, Seattle, Washington

A Case of the Blues — Or Not

"As an urban chicken consultant, I help people raise chickens and provide emergency care for their backyard flocks. A few months ago, a man called to tell me that his chicken was sick. He described the symptoms over the phone but they were pretty generic: fluffed, not eating, and staying in the coop all the time. I asked him if he could go to the coop. He said yes, and so I had him do a quick check-up on the chicken. I directed him to check for the most readily seen symptoms of common illnesses, and he did so, reporting to me what he was seeing and feeling. This effort turned up nothing.

Finally, I heard the chicken clucking in the background, and I said, 'Hold the phone up to the chicken. I want to hear the noise she's making.' He did so, and I knew immediately what the problem was. Laughing, I said, 'She's broody! Put a few eggs under her, and when they don't hatch in 21 days, she'll get sick of it and leave!'"

—*Jennifer Murtoff, Chicago, Illinois*

Mike "The Chicken Man" Goes to the Big City

Years ago, Mike Stanton traveled to Columbus, Ohio, for a chicken show. He arrived at his hotel late at night with 10 chickens in tow. One of the roosters he planned to show the next day had gotten dirty during the trip. Mike did what any bird fancier would do. He gathered up the rooster, took him into the hotel with him and cleaned him up. Because it was cold outside, Mike kept him in the hotel room for a few hours to dry. The next morning, Mike awoke to crowing. He had fallen asleep waiting for the rooster to dry. Mike quickly grabbed the rooster and headed out the door. Another guest who had heard the crowing and noticed Mike's Idaho license plate, chuckled and said, "You're from Idaho... huh?" To which Mike responded, "...yeah, I haven't been off the farm in 35 years... and I don't own an alarm clock!"

—*Mike Stanton, Weiser, Idaho*

Dogs as Chicken Sitters? Not!

Lastly, from our own chicken experience, here is a story reminiscent of Aesop's Fables.

As the door opened on the garage, we gently rolled in and

parked. Maggie jumped out of the car and immediately went to the single door in the garage that leads to the backyard. The last few nights, our "garage chickens" who had been free ranging out back, had huddled next to the door as they knew that through that space is where they needed to go to get to their roost. "Mom!" Maggie yelled. "Something's wrong with Thelma." I was just getting out of the car and rushed over to see what the fuss was about.

Thelma was covered in blood. Her neck feathers had been plucked. There was a gaping hole on the back of her neck and she was wet from head-to-toe. Thelma was in shock. We scooted the three other girls into their brooding box and I called Zamzows' chicken expert, Mike Stanton. It's a wonderful thing to have your own chicken professional within a couple of rings of a cell phone. Mike told me to keep Thelma separated from the other pullets, to clean her and apply Neosporin to the wound. Quietly, I was convinced she wasn't going to make it through the night. She was the sweetest of all the pullets. She was the one who would poke her head up first and look over the brooding box when we would enter the garage. She seemed to connect with us better than the other chickens. I felt awful. I had left the dogs in the backyard to "protect" the girls while we had dinner and ran errands. I had messed up.

I did as Mike instructed. I placed Thelma in an extra dog crate we had and hoped her state of shock wouldn't claim her during the night. We awoke the next morning and to our astonishment, Thelma was still alive. There was a collective sigh of relief — even from our other daughter, Helen, who doesn't much care for the chickens. We went about our morning. As my husband and I sat down to eat our breakfast, we saw Harley, our German Shepherd, sitting on our hot tub just outside the window. Beaujie, our Bichon Frise, was also on the hot tub. She was about a week into her season. I was "resting her" — not wanting to have summer puppies to care for. When all of the sudden we witnessed something quite peculiar. Beaujie, being a little "randy," had her paws on Harley's back and she was (how shall I say it?) "doing him?" All the while, she was pulling out tufts of fur with her teeth.

My husband and I looked at each other with a sense of realization. That explained it. We now knew how Thelma had been plucked. That made a lot of sense. Beaujie and Harley could kill a chicken in no time flat — if they really wanted.

All this occurred just before we were to leave for our oldest daughter's wedding in Florida. Our dear friends had agreed to take care of all our life forms. That included the dog in heat and the convalescing chicken, who by the way made a miraculous recovery. Our friends who cared for our animal menagerie informed us that while we were gone, Beaujie took an unnatural and strong liking to their house cat and did unspeakable things. There is a moral to this story. In fact, several we suspect.

—G.A.

CHAPTER 2

You Can Raise Chickens in Virtually Any Backyard

So you're thinking about putting chickens in your backyard. How much space do you need? Where will you keep them? Will they free range or will you keep them in a run on a roof in some big city? It depends on several factors. Make sure there is enough space in your yard or area for a coop that will give them shelter and plenty of freedom to move about. Also, stake out a spot that is free from regular watering.

The number of chickens you will keep essentially depends upon the space you have available and how large a coop you desire. The rule is to have at least two or more hens because of the unusual social dynamics of chickens. Chickens are NOT solitary animals. They are flock animals — they need at least one other chicken.

If you are considering a rooster, the rule of thumb is to have one rooster for 10 hens. You need a rooster for fertilized eggs. If you have a backyard flock for the purpose of egg production, you do not need a rooster. Hens will lay regardless.

> "My family and I raise 12 or so chickens. My mom stays at our little farmhouse, and cares for our animals when we travel. I noticed a tennis racket in the coop upon our return from a recent trip. I asked my mom about it and she said she never goes into the coop without the tennis racket in her hand because she is afraid of the rooster."
>
> —Dr. Tom Potisk, Caledonia, Wisconsin

It has been said over and over again, "If you want to upset your neighbors, get a rooster." They can be aggressive and they don't only crow at dawn, they crow all day long as they want to establish their territory. It's much like a dog marking his territory. Most roosters will also protect their hens. If you by chance have two roosters there will likely be a cockfight when they reach maturity.

> **Misconception #1:**
> You do NOT need a rooster to get eggs from your hens. Hens will lay eggs regardless of having a rooster.

Check with your city or county to see if either has restrictions on keeping chickens before you build or purchase a chicken coop. It is also a nice courtesy to let your neighbors know of your plans. I did this and I regularly supply them with fresh, free-range eggs and everyone is happy! Most cities and counties that allow backyard hens have a set-back rule for where you place your coop. Make certain you learn what that is and comply. It is a lot of work to build and set up your coop — only to learn it is too close to a neighbor's house or the property line. Since most people who keep backyard chickens don't have a rooster, they don't have to worry about the noise a rooster can make. However, hens can be quite noisy when they lay eggs. Either before or after the act, they often announce their plans to anyone within earshot. Once they have laid their egg, they get very excitable (as it should be) and can be quite boisterous. This is where being a good neighbor really counts, and communication is essential. Let your neighbors know that the noise they hear is your hen's natural "egg timer." The hens are simply announcing they've laid an egg — and fortunately, the excitement only lasts about 30-seconds.

Free Ranging vs. Cooped

Free ranging your chickens can be terrific. They (and you) get the benefits of going after insects, eating weeds and randomly fertilizing whatever is in their path. There are drawbacks however. You have to know they will ingest whatever you apply to your lawn, bushes and trees. If this concerns you, coop your chickens. There is control in a cooped hen.

There are proponents of keeping your chickens cooped so as to confine the chicken manure that is produced. Actually, this makes for easier clean up. Mike Stanton, chicken expert at Idaho's Zamzows says it's a better way to keep your chickens, "then you don't have to worry about what the birds will ingest, and there won't be chicken droppings all over your patio."

What about your pets? Will your dog chase the chickens? Will your cat be licking her chops? If you integrate your pets with the chickens early, there should be a natural ease to them co-existing in your backyard. Barriers such as exercise pens that can be placed in your yard, keep the chickens safe while the other pets get a chance to "check out" the new addition to your family.

CHAPTER 3

Pickin' Your Chicken

There is nothing cuter than fluffy, Ping-Pong ball sized chicks on Easter morning. My parents were very consistent with this tradition. My siblings and I would get four baby chicks every Easter. This was back when farm stores offered chicks with feathers that had been dyed green, pink and orange. The lucky ones were natural — yellow. They literally looked like little Easter eggs. Thankfully, that old practice is rare and illegal is some states. From the Easter chicks we received as kids, we were lucky if two survived the first week. Youngsters are overly curious and under cautious when it comes to baby chicks.

The practice of dying chicks is no longer popular.

Choosing the right chick for your situation is easy as long as you know what you want. Your local farm store will likely have chicks by early March. The sage advice is that you spend a little extra money (usually \$0.50–\$1.00 each) purchasing "sexed chicks." These are chicks that have either been born with pre-determined female genetic markers, such as a gold or black Sex Link, or, some keen eye-sighted professional in a hen house determined the sex of your little chicken. If you purchase straight run, or non-sexed chicks, you take a chance of getting all males. If you want roosters, this is acceptable. If you don't, sexed chicks are the way to go.

"We live in Fayetteville, Arkansas, in the middle of town. Fayetteville started allowing backyard chickens last year. We went to the farm store and got four New Hampshire Reds and one Silver Laced Wyandotte (black and white), all were supposed to be females. Roosters are not allowed in our town.

Our three kids (3, 4 and 6) named the black chick 'Darth Maul,' from Star Wars. We had a great time watching our chicks grow up.

Darth Maul always seemed to be the leader, the alpha chicken. One morning in June, our fears were realized. At 5:31 A.M. we heard a tentative "cock-a-doodle-doo." The next morning at the exact same time, we heard the same but with a bit more confidence.

I thought it was charming but I knew our neighbors might not agree. We sent Darth to live on a farm outside of town."

—Rolf Wilkin, Fayetteville, Arkansas

Some breeds of chickens make better backyard flocks. If you are looking for good laying hens that aren't "flighty" and can become a fun addition to your family, ask for advice from your local farm and garden store. Zamzows recommends Rhode Island Reds or Whites, Sex Links, Plymouth Rocks, Wellsummers, Marans or Ameraucanas, just to name a few.

Terminology:
Layers: the hens that lay an egg a day — or close to that.
Setters: the hens that lay and set on the eggs until they hatch (which takes 21-days).
Fryers: the chickens that gain weight rapidly and are butchered and thrown in — well, the fryer!

Bantams are the cute, smaller chickens. However, they are not the best egg layers. Standard breed or large fowl chickens are what most people have in their backyard flocks. For the layers, egg color runs the spectrum from white to dark brown. There are even hens that lay blue or green eggs. The so-called "Easter Egg Chickens" are the Ameraucana and Araucana that produce green and blue colored eggs. But, if you are looking for the trifecta in laying, setting and potential fryers, then a Barnevelder (which lays a dark brown egg) is a winner. However, most backyard chicken keepers I've met rarely turn members of their flock into Sunday dinner.

I purchased our little backyard flock just in time for Easter. I chose a gold and a black Sex Link, a Rhode Island White and a Lakenvelder. We later added a nice little Rhode Island Red to the flock. Other than the integration of the Rhode Island Red (establishing pecking order), they are all nice birds and get along well. Our favorites are definitely the Sex Links. The kids named them Thelma and Louise. They are quirky, friendly and great layers. In other parts of the country they are referred to as Black or Gold Star chickens or Black and Gold Buffs. They are a hybrid of a red male chicken crossed with a

Thelma and Louise foraging for bugs.

white or barred female. For instance, breeding a Rhode Island Red male and a Delaware female makes a gold Sex Link. By crossing a Rhode Island Red male and a Barred Plymouth Rock female you get a black Sex Link.

While your local farm and garden stores are great resources for chicks, you may also find spring chicks in your local newspaper classifieds or online classifieds such as Craigslist. In our area, Craigslist often has mature hens for sale. If you don't want to bother with raising the chicks, this may be the way to go. Expect to pay $10 to $25 for a mature laying hen. If you are interested in adopting, check the online pet website Petfinders. Put in your zip code and then select "bird" from the drop down pet menu.

Names:

A chick is a baby chicken that has not yet reached the age of laying (usually 20–24 weeks). A pullet is a chicken that is laying but has not passed her first birthday or experienced a moult. A hen is an adult female chicken, 12-months or older.

Editor's note: for this exercise, chickens are mostly referred to as chickens, hens or girls.

One other way to get your chicks is to mail-order them. Seriously, they will come to you via the United States Postal Service. Marilyn Doerr, an organic farmer who lives in Novelty, Ohio, (about 80 miles from Cleveland), orders her chicks from

Marilyn Doerr's mail-order Polish rooster Elvis.

McMurray Hatchery out of Webster City, Iowa. "The minimum order is 25 chicks," said Doerr. "They come to me in a cardboard box and they are healthy, happy little chicks. They stay warm because they are pretty snug in that one box." Doerr orders her chicks through McMurray because she likes their business practices and believes she's getting the healthiest chicks her money can buy. The cost is about $1.90 per sexed chick. She orders through a catalogue (you can also order online), and they are delivered in overnight mail. "It's great when the post office calls to tell me my mail is making 'peeping' noises!" adds Doerr. Her favorites are Australorp, Araucana and Barred Rock chickens. She raises the hens on her small farm and sells the organic eggs at a farmer's market and to her neighbors.

Egg Color and Chicken Breed

- **Dark brown:** Barnevelder, Marans, Rhode Island, Sex Link, Welsummer

- **Light brown:** Brahma, Buff Orpington, Plymouth Rock, Sex Link, Wyandotte

- **White:** Buff Minorca, Golden Campine, Leghorn, Silver Lakenvelder

- **Blue or blue-green:** Ameraucana, Araucana

CHAPTER 4

Keeping Baby Chicks Safe

Keeping your baby chicks safe and warm requires some set-up. The chicks will live in what is called a "brooder box." A wading pool, a cardboard box or an old bathtub make good brooders. Or, you can purchase a commercial brooder box. Whichever you decide, make certain to keep a wire lid on the box for ample airflow and to prevent flight. Baby chicks can obtain loft at a very early age. Your brooder box will need water, a feeder, bedding and a heat source. To start, keep the chicks warm at 95°. A 250-watt infrared heat lamp is recommended. Your brooder

Brooder box example / Marilyn Doerr.

needs to be big enough that the chicks can benefit from the heat lamp but also get away from heat. A thermometer placed at "chick level" is best for determining the brooder temperature. As the chicks mature, you can drop the brooder temperature by 5° each week. Be certain to place the heat lamp in a safe area where it won't catch fire to the brooder or the bedding.

Temperature for Brooder Box	
Age of Chick	Degrees/Fahrenheit
1 Week	90-95
2 Weeks	85-90
3 Weeks	80-85
4 Weeks	75-80
5 Weeks	70-75
6 Weeks +	70

If you have many chicks they will keep each other warm and your brooder box temperature can be reduced by a few degrees. If your chicks reach 6-weeks of age and your outside temperature is 70°, it's time to move them from the brooder to the coop. If the outside temperature has not reached 70°, keep them in your brooder until it warms. If you are brooding your chicks in a cardboard box, you can always add another box as the chicks mature to provide more room. Baby chicks need a half square foot each of space and by the time they are 6-weeks old, make certain each chick has nearly a square foot of space.

Chicks must always have fresh water and plenty of food available. Put the food, called Chick Starter, in the cool part of the brooder. It is best to spend a little money on specially designed chick waterers and feeders, otherwise, you run the risk of wasting a lot of Chick Starter and having dirty water that gets spilled.

Thelma and Louise still like their chick fount and feeder.

The material you put in the bottom of your brooder should be something that you can keep clean. A clean environment prevents your chicks from getting sick. Avoid anything that could be slick. For this reason plain

Thelma and Louise in a cardboard brooder box.

newspaper is not recommended. If a chick steps in droppings on a slick surface, there is risk of injury. Zamzows recommends a deep layer of wood pellets. The binding component in the pellet is non-toxic and it makes the floor of your brooder easy to keep clean. Other bedding possibilities are: chopped straw, wood shavings (no cedar or redwood) or sawdust. Clean the bedding often. Make certain your brooder bedding is non-toxic and watch your chick to be assured they ingest only Chick Starter. This is why Zamzows recommends the affordable, wood pellets — they make good bedding and the pellets are too large for the chicks to eat.

Most chicks figure out how to roost at about 4–6 weeks of age. In chicken lingo a roost is both a noun and a verb. The noun version is an above ground, horizontal surface on which they sleep. You might also refer to it as a perch. It is important they take to roosting (the verb version), early. Place a roost (away from the heat) in the brooding box for this purpose. I cut two holes on either side of the heavy cardboard box and slipped a wooden 1x2 slat through the holes. I put the 2" side horizontally so the chicks had plenty of roost to feel comfortable. To accommodate the roosting chicks, I also had to fashion a higher enclosure. I did this by using the door off of a dog kennel and some old screening material I had in the garage. It created an A-frame roof. It didn't look pretty, but it worked. We kept our chicks in the garage until they were about 10-weeks old. We waited longer to move them outdoors because we had a particularly cold, wet spring. By and large, a chick can be placed in an outdoor coop at 6–8 weeks of age — as long as the weather isn't too severe and the temperature is above 70°.

Make certain your brooder is placed where there are no drafts and is safe from predators. Even the sweetest Bichon Frise cannot be trusted when out of site and near a brooding box. I learned this the hard way.

Huey, the champion-bred Bichon Frise stud I was keeping for my mom the breeder, accidentally got stuck in the garage after our 11-year-old daughter went out to fetch something from the refrigerator. She didn't know he had followed her. About 45 minutes later there was a terrible racket.

We found Huey near the brooder and Peep, our little Rhode Island White, was dead. There wasn't blood or little chick feathers in the area — we assumed Huey broke her neck. I raced out to Zamzows and purchased another Rhode Island White chick for our daughter. I found one about the same age as Peep. We told the kids what happened when they returned home from school. Huey was REALLY in the dog house, the new chick became Peep II, and we all learned a valuable lesson.

—G.A.

CHAPTER 5

Home Sweet Home

Your chickens need a coop in which to roost, lay eggs and be protected from predators. Cooping your chickens is the single biggest aspect of keeping hens in your backyard. There is no "right way" to coop your birds. However, there are aspects of cooping that should go into your plan and there are coop features to avoid.

Building a coop can be a great family project. There are countless plans on the internet. You should plan spending a weekend or two to get the project completed. We chose our chicks and they stayed in the brooder box for 10 weeks before we set up a coop. So, between the time when you get your chicks and the time they are old enough to be cooped, you can figure out a coop that best fits your needs.

The "All Cooped Up" tour, Adine Storer, Belmont, Massachusetts.

Those who keep chickens on larger pieces of property will tell you they use an old shed, a former dog house or even an old vanity or dresser to coop their chickens. Whatever you choose, build or buy a coop that will protect your chickens from predators. If your community offers a coop tour don't miss it. It's the best way to get innovative ideas on how to coop your hens in your own backyard.

Remember to pick a location in your yard that is secure, away from sprinklers and with careful consideration of nearby neighbors.

Mike Stanton also suggests you consider your climate, and whether you want a southern (for cold climates) or northern (for hot climates) exposure.

> *"We love our chickens, but our neighbors don't! We incubated seven eggs about eight months ago. Five adorable chicks hatched. My husband built a 'Taj-Ma-Coop' for them almost on the property line of our one acre parcel. We never knew that our neighbors' bedroom window was just on the other side of the fence dividing our two houses. We quickly discovered that we had three roosters that were waking our neighbors long before we awoke in our bedroom ... way on the other side of our property. Now we are down to two hens, hoping to incubate some more eggs. No recent complaints from neighbors though."*
>
> —Julie Arnheim, Los Altos Hills, California

Your coop will require a nesting box. If you have four or more hens, it's advisable to have two nesting boxes.

The Poop Coop, Jim Schwartz, Parma, Idaho.

The standard nesting box-to-hen ratio is quite high: a minimum of one nesting box per seven hens. Your hens will be more comfortable if you provide a lower ratio. Mike Stanton keeps four hens to one nesting box. Afford ample room for them to move about.

Chickens need at least 3–4 square feet of coop space (per bird) to maintain quality of life and health. Remember the old saying, "A chicken comes home to roost?" Well, it's true. Chickens always return to their last known spot for roosting at night. To roost or perch is how chickens turn in for the night. When they roost, it keeps them from becoming prey to external parasites, large predators, and it keeps them from sleeping in their droppings. Hens generally prefer the highest roost possible. It's a survival instinct.

Roosting hen next to a contemporary coop. Mitchell Snyder, Portland, Oregon.

If you live in a cold climate, Mike Stanton recommends you use a 2x4 wooden board set on its wide side on which the hens will roost. This way, when temperatures drop below freezing, the hens won't freeze their toes. They roost with their breast feathers covering their feet — thus insulating them from the cold. There isn't a whole lot you can do for their combs. Some hen keepers say to coat the combs with petroleum jelly and that will protect them from getting frostbitten. Mike Stanton also recommends that if the lower part of your coop has 1" poultry netting/chicken wire, that you should add some sort of site barrier to the coop. This can be easily accomplished by using burlap or weed-block hardware cloth. This will keep other animals from spooking your little flock.

The Poop Coop exterior, Jim Schwartz, Parma, Idaho.

There are pre-fabricated coops that you can order and assemble yourself. You can order them online or from your local farm store. Often they are smaller coops that are simple in design. Make certain you will be able to easily get into and out of the coop to clean it.

If you have more money than time, have a coop built for you. The cost is higher — about $700+. There are builders who customize coops for clients. If you go this route, you can specify exactly what you want and need. There are many custom coop builders on the internet. We found a builder right in our hometown. His story fascinated me.

Bill Finnigan is a coop builder in demand. Finnigan made his living remodeling bathrooms and kitchens. But when the economy went south in 2007 and he couldn't get enough work to feed his family, he turned to his pastor. His pastor told him that this "chicken thing" was growing and why not try his hand at building chicken coops? Finnigan started with a converted dog house and evolved his plans from there. Now, he builds coops all over the west. Some of the coops he builds are from his simple plans, some are more elaborate. A good number of his chicken coops even have an exclusive California zip code!

The MJ Coop, Bill Finnigan, Boise, Idaho.

Once you have your coop, the next step is to determine what type of bedding you need for below the roost, in the nesting boxes and in the bottom of the coop (if necessary). Straw is a good choice. It's relatively cheap and is absorbent. Dried grass clippings are even cheaper and make good nesting material. Just be certain that whatever you apply to your lawn is all-natural as the hens may try to eat some of the bedding. The same materials you use in a brooder box: straw, pine shavings (no cedar or redwood), wood or paper pellets can be used in a coop. Shredded paper (as long as it's not slick) can also be used. When cleaning out your coop, place old bedding material in your composter or compost pile. Mike Stanton advises to NOT use ground corn cobs as bedding. Chickens will eat ground cobs and will not be able to digest it, effectively killing them.

Cleaning the Coop:
Use a bucket and metal tongs to "harvest" the nitrogen-rich chicken droppings from below your chicken roost. Try to do this every other day. Throw the chicken manure directly into the composter or compost pile. This prolongs the life of the straw placed in the bottom of the roosting part of the coop. Make sure to "turn" or mix up the straw very well after the harvesting. A clean coop makes for healthy chickens!

Having clean water is the most important nutrient for your chickens. A plastic watering fount is great for chicks and pullets

Fount placed on popcorn tin heater keeps water from freezing during winter months.

(young hens). However, once the plastic wears out, purchase a galvanized steel fount. If cared for properly, this will last you a lifetime. Place the water just high enough for the smallest hen to be able to drink from the trough, usually at the height level of the hen's back. By elevating the water, hens who scratch the ground near the waterer will not be able to flick dirt, rocks or bedding into the trough.

Winter in colder climates poses a problem in keeping the water from freezing. You must either purchase a water fount heater or make one. Our heater is made with a simple, metal Christmas popcorn tin and a shop light with a 60-watt bulb. The rim of the tin has a v-notch in it so the cord can run out and the lid can be secured. The maker of this heater, my husband, said the best part of putting it together was eating the popcorn.

When your chicks graduate from the brooder box to the coop, you'll likely need a larger feeder. Choose a feed-

Hanging hen feeder with plastic cake cover keeps the feed clean and dry.

er that will accommodate the number of hens you have. Many of them feature adjustable feed levels. It is also advisable to get the feeders with the anti-scratch vanes. They help prevent crowding and feed waste.

Hang the feeder in the coop where it will be protected from rain. You also should place it so the feed trough is at the same height level as the back of your smallest chicken. Put only feed in this trough. If you mix in Chicken Scratch (cracked corn), or oyster shell (for added calcium and to harden the shells of the eggs your hens lay), the chickens will search out what they want and the rest will fall to the ground. My chickens occasionally roost on the steps leading from the run to the coop. I use the top of a store-bought cake container to keep them from fouling their own food. I put a slit in the top of a plastic lid and slipped it onto the top of the feeder. It works like a charm.

If you plan to free range your chickens, it's a good idea to keep them cooped for the first several days before letting them out. This way they will know and become accustomed to where they roost, where their nesting boxes are and where they get their food and water.

Be certain to secure the coop at night as many nocturnal predators will be interested in your hens. Specifically, raccoons and skunks seem to cause the most havoc with backyard chickens. Raccoons are very clever and can often unlatch a chicken coop. They can also reach into a coop that has large enough openings or doesn't have the 1" chicken wire and try to pull a chicken through the wire. Chicken wire is constructed with openings at 1" (or smaller) for this reason — it deters predators from reaching in and grabbing hold.

Deterring predators:

"I brush our German Shepherd and use the fur in our chicken coop. I clean all the fur from the brushes and then mix it in with the chicken's bedding. I've even mixed a little fur in the dirt and straw around the coop. It's my belief, the nocturnal predators get one whiff of the fur and they don't want to go near the coop! We even have a raccoon living in a nearby tree and it hasn't given us any trouble."

-April Baker, Meridian, Idaho

Here are several photos of coops taken by backyard chicken keepers. All of them were eager to share how they have incorporated hen houses into their backyard decor.

Is that a coop or a play house? You decide! Pahlee Bretoi, Eugene, Oregon.

The Flockers, super tractor. Mary & RD Benion, Palo, Iowa.

A three drawer bathroom vanity is turned upside down, a roof is added and put on wooden legs to make a humble coop. What was the top drawer, is now flipped to create a slide out nesting box.
Graham Paterson, Boise, Idaho.

A simple, portable "chicken tractor." Land's Sake Farms, Weston, Massachusetts.

Mitchell Snyder Architect coop. Portland, Oregon.

The one coop I came across in my research that really caught my eye was in Oregon. It was designed and built by Portland architect, Mitchell Snyder. My tastes are more contemporary — so maybe that is why his backyard coop appeals to me. It reminds me of my college art lessons on Frank Lloyd Wright's architectural designs. I marveled at how lucky Mitch's chickens are to live in such a nice structure. I wondered about the ventilation and how the run was attached and whether the chickens had much daylight. Here are some of the questions I fired at Mitch:

GA: How easy is it to clean?

MS: The coop is fairly easy to clean, but it's actually the one big change I'd make to the design. It'd be better to have a tray that could slide out from the outside of the hen house, removed, and easily emptied into our compost bin.

GA: Are the girls protected from the rainy Oregon weather while at the same time getting plenty of ventilation?

MS: The hens are extremely well protected against our wet and cold winters. Before adding the exterior cladding (reclaimed cedar siding from our local reclaimed building material store, The Rebuilding Center), we added, to the walls of the coop, the leftover insulation we had from insulating our house. In the winter, we also insert a fabric flap over the opening between the hen house and the run. We cut slits into it (similar to the plastic flaps you see in a grocery store that lead into refrigerated rooms) so that the hens can pass through. When it gets near or below freezing we have a ceramic heater that screws in like a light socket. In addition to keeping the hens warm, it keeps their water from freezing. I'd also say it's an argument against building a gigantic hen house that is bigger than needed for the number of hens you have. A smaller tightly sealed hen house is easier to keep warm.

In the summer, there are the two upper windows that open for ventilation. The longer door on the bottom is the access to the egg box. Around the corner is another small vent. The green roof also helps absorb the most intense summer heat.

GA: Do the girls free range or do they stay in the fenced run?

MS: The hens have access to the run from the hen house. The run is a frame of cedar 2x2's and completely enclosed with wire mesh. We also had to dig down six inches and bury wire mesh under the soil in the run so that no predators or rodents could burrow down, under, and into it. We let them out as much as possible in our yard to free range, but due to predators (mainly raccoons here in Portland), we have to be home to keep an eye on them. We have inherited two hens from a neighbor's flock. They were attacked by raccoons. I have worried about the many outdoor cats we have in our neighborhood, but so far none has approached the hens when they are in the yard.

Native sedum.

GA: How does the planter, in the top, drain? And, what exactly is growing in it?

MS: The roof looks flat, but under the soil the roof is pitched to drain to a gutter and downspout on the back side. The plants are native sedums that do not require much water during the long stretches between rains in the summer months.

View from above.

GA: Your coop seems very contemporary and "upper crust." Did you ever contemplate a "plain old coop?"

MS: The hens' comfort and protection (both from the elements and predators) were the most important considerations. From there we tried to place the hen house and run with consideration of our neighbors. The height of the hen house and run were determined by the height of the fence to keep it obscured from view. With those requirements, as an architect, it became an interesting design experiment. The aesthetics were in line with any other project I've done, keeping it as simple as possible.

You can see more of Mitch's great coop photos at www.msnyderarch.com.

CHAPTER 6

Free Ranging
in the Backyard

My sister looked at me with her "I can't believe you just said that" look. "Really, you call it free ranging?" Jody asked.

"Yes," I said. "The girls actually prefer it."

"You mean they are 'loose'…as in 'loose in your backyard?' Like your dogs? Are you free ranging your dogs?"

Unlike dogs, chickens that free range help control pests. They eat a mixed and bountiful diet of weeds and they fertilize wherever they walk. If you free range your hens, make certain the area is secure from predators, including your dog and the neighborhood dogs. If your dog is not chicken-friendly, do not free range your chickens.

Chicken keepers who free range their birds will tell you all sorts of stories about the hens and their inquisitive and quirky nature. They also marvel at the social interaction between the hens.

The girls free ranging in the backyard.

Worried about getting your chickens back into the coop at night? Don't worry. Your hens are creatures of habit. They will make their way back to their roost in the coop as it gets dark. There may be a few non-conforming hens though, who are not as smart as the others, and they will make it back "somewhere near" the coop.

We have a Silver Lakenvelder, Henrietta or "Hank," routinely roosts atop the coop. For some reason she doesn't follow the other girls into the coop and she charts her own course. Closing up the coop at night has become a two-person job, one person to hold the flashlights, the other to spot and capture Hank. We then place her in the run to find her way up to the coop to roost. Incidentally, of the five hens we have, Hank is the least kid friendly, flighty and not too bright. But, she is a champion layer with very hard shelled eggs and she will take on the dogs — letting them know, she's not a hen to mess with. I give her personality points for this.

Hank, the wayward Lakenvelder.

Free-range chickens will eventually find their way to the nesting boxes when it's time to lay an egg. Keep them cooped for a while before they are about to produce eggs and this will deter them from nesting somewhere in your yard. Zamzows' Mike Stanton warned me about this and I was under the impression the girls (who had started laying) were all compliant in using the nesting boxes in the coop. That was until we had a family clean-up day in the yard and moved the trailer to haul some trimmings to the landfill. Underneath the trailer we found a nest with a dozen multi-colored eggs in it. There was no telling how long the nest had been there so we had to throw out the eggs. From that point, we kept the girls in the coop a little later each day. Now, they are all using the nesting boxes daily.

The wonderful thing about free ranging your hens is they get a varied diet. They eat greens, consume protein-rich bugs and find other tidbits around the yard. Chickens will eat just about anything. If you use herbicides and pesticides on your lawn that are unsafe, the chickens will ingest that and it will show up in egg production. That is why, if you free range your flock, you should apply only all-natural products to your lawn, plants and trees. If you are a gardener, chickens will feast on your early crops in the spring, making a meal out of your tender, young lettuce starts.

An old chicken farmer to my restaurateur husband, "Could I get a container in which to take my steak home?"

"Certainly," my husband obliges. "Looks like lunch tomorrow."

"No," says the old chicken farmer. "I feed it to my hens. They'll pert near eat anything ... that won't eat them first!"

Free range chickens are also able to pick up tiny pieces of rock called "grit." Chickens don't have teeth, so the grit helps in the breakdown and digestion of food. You will notice on your hens there is a bulge on the right side of their breast. This is their "crop." The crop is a temporary storage area at the base of the hen's neck. The food is mixed with acids and other digestive enzymes in the crop and gizzard. Grit in the gizzard is used to grind the food so the hens can digest it and benefit from the nutrients. The grit, along with the food they consume, passes through the chicken's digestive system. If you don't free range your birds, make certain to provide them grit. You can purchase it at your local farm and garden store. Remember not to mix it in with the chicken feed in the feeder. Fashion a rabbit feeder in your coop in which to dispense the grit.

You might also want to clip your hen's wings so they don't fly into the neighbor's trees. It's usually a two-person job. Clip a wing on one side only, so if the hen attempts flight, she is thrown off-balance. If you do both wings the hen will still be able to achieve loft.

On a chickens' wing, there are three layers of feathers. Cut through the middle row of the primary feathers. This will prevent your hens from visiting the neighbors across the fence and potentially ending up in their dog's mouth or on their dinner table.

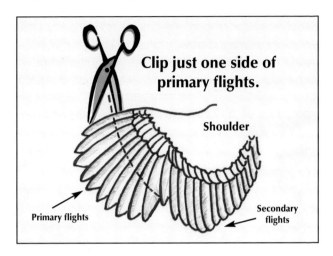

Clip just one side of primary flights.

Shoulder

Primary flights

Secondary flights

Words of caution: do not cut any new growth feathers with blood in the shaft (blood feathers). You will notice a difference in these feathers as they appear to have a pink hue to them. With our black Sex Link, we have to hold her next to a bright light or in the sun to be absolutely certain we are not cutting new growth.

The Dirty Details

One other free ranging issue chicken keepers encounter is the poop. There is a lot of it. It is hard to control and a challenge to keep your yard clean. I clean up our yard like I clean up dog waste. The only difference is, I put the chicken manure in the composter and send the dog waste to the landfill. I'm very cautious not to mix up the two. It's a big job to clean up the yard. By using long-handled, metal restaurant tongs, a plastic bucket and a plastic bag, I can clean our 1/3 acre in about a 1/2 hour — as long as I stay on top of it.

> **Fun Fowl Facts:**
> One hen will provide you with 25 pounds of chicken manure annually!

I have also taken to using a wire brush and water to clean the more liquid chicken poop from the patio. If you are not right on top of it, some chicken poop will begin to dry in the hot sun making it harder to remove. Additionally it will freeze in the winter time and is very difficult to remove in cold weather. These practices alone move some chicken keepers to coop their little flocks full-time. The mess is confined to the coop and is easier to clean.

If your chickens don't have a big enough area wherein to free range, build them a secure pen with plenty of space so they can enjoy clean air and get exercise. Just remember to provide 3–4 square feet per bird.

Potential Hazards of "Free Ranging"

"My spoiled pet Plymouth Rock, Loretta, lives in our suburban Virginia backyard. During nice weather, we spend time in the garden together. One February, a hawk swooped down and gouged her back. Feathers flew everywhere. I raced out to

Loretta with HenSaver Jacket.

get her and my heart sank. She had two serious deep gashes on either side of her body.

I went online and visited backyard chicken forums and did some speedy research on avian first aid. I followed a veteran farmer's step-by-step guide and rinsed the wounds with peroxide and dabbed on Neosporin. Then I put Loretta in a box and brought her inside the house and worried. My husband and I started talking about whom and how we would put her down if she didn't recover. I kept treating her every day, though my stomach flipped at the sight of the injuries. After a few weeks she was definitely on the road to recovery.

But that old hawk still patrols the neighborhood — so I bought her a HenSaver jacket online. It has embroidered eyes on the back to deter attacks. It looks ridiculous, but I don't want to lose my gardening buddy!"

—Melissa Sinclair, Richmond, Virginia

CHAPTER 7

Egg Production

It is cliché, but there really isn't anything that beats farm-fresh eggs. Our children marveled at how clean and warm the eggs were the first time they gathered them from the coop. The appearance, taste and freshness are of a higher quality than that from a store bought egg. Baking with the fresh eggs is a joy and really brings out a recipe.

Eggs come in a myriad of colors.

About the time your hens are 20–24 weeks old, they will begin laying eggs. When they first start laying, it may be sporadic. You will find the eggs are of varying sizes and at times, you may even get a soft, non-shelled egg. Don't be alarmed. This is just your chicken trying to get "into the swing of things." When we get one of these, we cook it, let it cool and treat the dogs to the egg. The eggs might come out speckled or even wrinkled. Consider it a lesson in nature — or nature's imperfections.

Though unfertilized eggs can remain fresh and unrefrigerated for up to two weeks, it's important to gather your eggs from the nesting boxes in a timely manner. If there are unattended eggs in the coop, an overly curious hen might peck at the eggs and subsequently eat them. You don't want this. I check my coop twice a day. Occasionally on the first check of the nesting boxes, I'll collect eggs from all or nearly all the hens. If this is the case, I won't have to check the nesting box again until I close the girls in for the night.

Little Known Fact:
Did you know that fresh-from-your-coop, unwashed, non-fertilized eggs don't need to be refrigerated? In fact they can remain unrefrigerated for up to 14-days without any sign of deterioration.

Also, when you crack open an egg and see the yolk, you may think the yolk would be the baby chick. It isn't. If it is a fertilized egg, it is the baby chick's food. You'll know an egg is fertilized by the presence of an opaque disc that appears on the yolk. The disc is the germ — or the beginning of the chick.

When the egg comes out of the chicken it is sanitary. So, it is important to keep the nesting boxes very clean. There is much debate over whether to wash an egg. A single egg comprises more than 8,000 pores. The argument is, if you wash the eggs you are removing the "bloom" from the egg — a natural protective coating. You'll also allow bacteria into the egg through the water and any cleaning agent you use.

Wash the egg only if you need to remove droppings or dirt. Since the bloom will be compromised on that egg — make certain to enjoy that one before the rest, as it won't hold up like the other non-washed eggs. If there is a bit of debris on the egg, flick it off with a small, stiff bristled brush. Many backyard chicken keepers will wash the bloom just prior to cooking the egg. They'll also "float" the eggs prior to washing and cooking. This is how you determine whether an egg is fresh. Place the egg in cool water. If the egg lies properly on its side underwater, you have a fresh egg. As an egg ages, air transfers through the pores of the shell and into the egg. This gives it buoyancy when placed in water. If an egg is listing a bit but not completely floating they are still edible. If an egg stands upright while still maintaining contact with the bottom of the bowl, this egg is officially old.

Keeping track of the eggs you gather is important so that you consume the older eggs first. This is easily accomplished by using a carton that will hold 18 eggs. Write an "O" (for older) on the left side of the carton and an "N" (for newer) on the right side of the carton. Move the eggs one-by-one to the left as they are used — making room for the fresher eggs to be placed on the "N" side. This is a great lesson in food rotation for kids — get them involved. Our family eats a lot of eggs. But occasionally, I'll have more eggs than the 18 spaces in my carton. That's when I offer a half dozen eggs to one of my six (across the fence) neighbors for supporting me in my backyard chicken experience. As I've said before, this goes a long way in creating good relations.

The size and color of your eggs depend upon the type of chicken you have. Bantams (smaller chickens) lay small to medium sized eggs. They also make good setters. We purposely stayed away from the cute, little Silkie bantams because we were more interested in egg production. The larger fowl, like our Sex Links and Rhode Island hens, will lay medium to extra large sized eggs. Occasionally you will get a monster egg. They generally have two yolks in them and are bigger than any extra large egg you've purchased at the market. We call these bonus eggs, and the kids are fascinated by them. Once your hen establishes a laying routine the eggs become more uniform in size. Our Lakenvelder, Hank, lays medium sized, off-white eggs. They are the hardest shelled eggs of the bunch. What she lacks in brains and friendliness, she makes up for in her egg production.

Did You Know?
The laying hen as we know it descended from the Red Jungle Fowl. In the wild, the Jungle Fowl laid only enough eggs to produce offspring. Over the centuries, farmers using science, bred hens so they would produce eggs daily.

Have you heard of the Easter Eggers? They are the Ameraucana and Araucana chickens that lay various shades of blue and green eggs. The Marans lay a dark, chocolate brown egg. And of course, the Leghorns (which are popular with commercial egg producers) lay a white shelled egg. There are also chickens that lay speckled eggs and an egg that is a light shade of pink. Except for a few breeds of chickens, you can usually tell the color of the eggs they will lay by their earlobes. If their lobes are white, they'll lay a white egg. If they are dark, they'll generally lay a brown egg. From our five hens, we gather eggs that are white, green and reddish-brown. They are gorgeous!

Thelma and Louise show their lobes.

A hen will likely lay an egg every 24–26 hours. They will be active layers for about three years. The natural life span of a chicken can be up to 15 years. However, 5–10 years is more common. Many backyard chicken keepers would never "process" their egg laying "pets" and throw them on the grill. But from a practical standpoint, there are people who do.

Chickens will periodically stop laying eggs during their "moulting" period. This is the time when they shed old feathers and grow new ones. Their bodies cannot lay eggs and moult at the same time. This is a natural occurrence that happens once a year for most laying hens. However, chicks go through one full, and three partial moults during maturity. Complete moulting occurs from 1–6 weeks of age. That's when they lose their soft downy feathers. Partial moulting

Moulting hen. Cassie Kauffman, www.lifetransplant.com

occurs at 7–9 weeks, 12–16 weeks and 20–22 weeks. During this final moult, the stiff tail feathers grow in.

Hens will go into a moult for several reasons. Shorter days in autumn can trigger a moult because of shortened feeding time and subsequent loss of body weight. Your hen can go into a moult because of fatigue or they have reached a completion of the laying cycle, as chickens lay eggs for a biologically pre-determined period of time. A moult rarely lasts longer than 12-weeks. During a moult, and because you won't be gathering and eating eggs, it's a good time for you to enjoy corn flakes.

Some backyard chicken keepers add artificial light to their coops to simulate long summer days. The more sunlight chickens have, the more regularly they lay. There is a lot of debate surrounding this as many people believe nature should just take its course. But when you take a realistic look, we don't let our birds simply fend for themselves. We provide them with a home, special food and supplements and any other necessity to keep them healthy and productive. The arguments surrounding the use of artificial light seem to center on adequate rest for the chickens. If you've been around chickens much, they rest when they need it.

If you choose to add artificial lighting, make certain to add it where the light is safe, free from potential harm to your birds, and cannot ignite a fire. There are inexpensive timers that will allow you to keep your hens in extended light in the winter. It's best to purchase a multi-setting timer. The timer turns the lights on for a few hours in the evening and then again in the morning for a couple hours before sunrise. For example, set your light to come on at 05:00 hours and off at 07:00. Then, have the light come back on in the evening at 17:00 and turn off at 19:00. The use of a multi-setting timer will save you money and keep your little flock producing.

CHAPTER 8

Taking Special Care of Your Chickens

Chickens are interesting creatures. For years, there have been theories that they were descended from dinosaurs. Just recently scientists at the Harvard Medical School participated in a study that showed conclusively that there are similarities between the DNA taken from the remains of a 68-million-year-old Tyrannosaurus rex and the bone collagen of chickens. This provides molecular support for the premise that your backyard chickens may indeed be decedents of dinosaurs.

T-rex or not, your little flock depends on you. Temperatures and elements can get the better of them. During the hot days of summer, you may notice your chickens with their mouths open as they nest, roost or free range. They are in fact panting in an effort to keep cool. Chickens are actually more vulnerable to heat than cold. Another benefit of free ranging your birds is they are very good at seeking out the cool spots in your yard. You will find they are skillful at scratching down to the cool ground to get relief from a hot

Chickens do OK in snow, but they are not fond of it.

climate. As always, cool clean water is essential to keeping healthy hens and helping them to regulate their body temperatures.

Winter temperatures in many parts of the United States pose great threats to chickens if the proper precautions aren't observed. Below freezing temperatures can cause frostbite on the combs and feet of your hens.

There isn't much you can do to protect the hen's comb except apply a thin coat of petroleum jelly. You can help protect the hen's feet by providing a roost that is 4" wide. A 2x4 wooden board works nicely for this. If the hen roosts on the 4" side of the board, she'll splay her toes and cover them with her breast feathers as she roosts at night. This prevents frost bitten toes during cold overnight temperatures.

Air flow within the coop is as vitally important in the winter as it is in the summer. If you attempt to keep the coop closed in the winter to conserve heat, you'll have a humid, unhealthy coop. Restricted ventilation leads to ammonia build-up in the air, which is bad for your hens. The rule-of-thumb is, if your coop smells worse inside than it does outside, your hens are suffering. Ventilate! Remember, during the winter your hens benefit from thick layers of feathers. But they have no natural resistance to reduced air quality and bacteria in the bedding.

If you free range your birds in the summer, do the same in the winter. However, I've yet to meet a chicken who really likes walking in snow. I personally keep the hens cooped until the snow melts and then I free range them. Exercise is a great way for the chickens to generate body heat. Providing your flock a feed that has a higher protein content in the winter is strongly advised. The protein level in your feed should be at 20% during the winter months. In reviewing your feed, Mike Stanton recommends to always purchase a feed that is a "fixed formula," meaning the manufacturers keep quality ingredients the same. If you go with a "least cost formula," the beneficial ingredients of your food changes with the economy.

Feed Guidelines:
6–8 weeks: Chick Starter
(has added protein for growth)

8–20 weeks: Pullet Developer (less protein)

20+ weeks: Lay Pellets at about 16% protein
(in winter months, increase to
20% protein in Lay Pellets)

Chickens generally won't eat once it gets dark. So, with winter's short days, they have a shorter window in which to forage. If your flock doesn't get enough to eat, the egg production drops off. It's a good idea to offer your girls some Chicken Scratch before they turn in on winter nights. Feeding them grains late in the day allows them to roost with a full crop. Their bodies metabolize the scratch during the night, thus boosting their calorie intake. Plus, you can generally get them back into the coop if they are familiar with hen scratch. Scattering scratch in the coop will get them inside for the evening and keeps your hens busy. Additionally, this will deter the girls from pecking each other out of boredom. Put only enough scratch in the run that the girls can consume within about 10 minutes. If the scratch is on the wet ground too long, it gets soggy and can mold.

Where do the eggs come from?

Really, where do they come from? It's called the vent. Actually, there is a lot going on with your chicken's vent. Truth be told, it's the area from where chicken waste and eggs come. It is also the reproductive channel. But, before you are totally grossed out, there is some really cool biology that is at work in the vent area. All birds have this common opening for reproduction and for elimination. Chickens don't have bladders. Their urine is not a fluid. It is a white paste called urates. You can see this if you do any harvesting of chicken droppings for your garden. The intestine and oviduct come together in a cavity called the cloaca. This is a rather dirty place. But, when an egg is laid, it is always clean and virtually sterile.

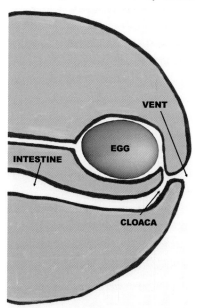

When a hen lays an egg she turns part of the cloaca and the last segment of the oviduct inside out. The egg emerges in such a way

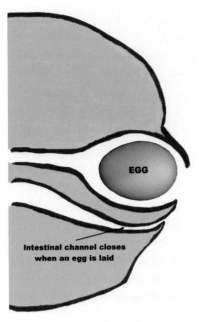

EGG

Intestinal channel closes when an egg is laid

that it cannot contact the walls of the cloaca and get contaminated. Additionally, the hen's intestine and inner part of the cloaca are kept shut by the emerging egg. Again, eggs are clean when they are laid — you just need to do your part in keeping your chicken's feet and nesting box tidy.

You also need to periodically check your chicken's vent. Feces can build up around the vent and prevent the bird from eliminating. This is called "pasty vent" or "pasty butt." If it is left unchecked, it can kill your chicken. For baby chicks, use a cotton swab and some warm water or mineral oil to clean the vent. For mature chickens, slip on a pair of rubber gloves and place your hen under some warm running water. Gently rub off the pasty area and check for parasites. Sanitize your work area afterward.

Pasty Vent and Chicks:
Don't attempt to bathe baby chicks with pasty vent. They are not mature enough and cannot regulate their body temperature.

A Well Groomed Hen

When I was a kid and we kept our Leghorn flock, the thought of trimming their toenails or beaks never occurred to us. The toe nails seemed to take care of themselves. The beaks were another case. I remember finding our rooster, Casanova, dead, on the ground. It looked like the hens had ganged-up on him as he appeared pecked to death. (Really, an awful site for a young girl to see!) Chickens will go after just about anything colored red. Who knows what happened to Casanova? As a young girl, I figured the hens had finally had enough of him and did him in. Had the hen's beaks been clipped, maybe he would have survived.

Most birds wear back their beaks by the natural act of eating and pecking around. Beak trimming is common in egg-laying breeds of chickens as a precautionary measure to decrease the incidence of cannibalism among large flocks. In small flocks of laying hens, pecking is usually not a problem. However, if you have a hen that shows aggressive tendencies, you might consider trimming her beak.

Instructions on Trimming Beaks and Toenails

First, ask someone for assistance. This is generally a two-person job. Sit on a chair in a room with good lighting. Place your trimming tools within reach. Put a towel over your lap to keep yourself clean and to wrap the hen in, if necessary. If you need to wrap your hen, gently wrap her in the towel like you would roll a burrito. This keeps them from flapping their wings while you are working.

Often you must hold her head, as most chickens don't like having their beaks clipped. Open her mouth gently, by pressing on the sides — similar to how you get dogs to open their mouths.

Using a dog or feline nail trimmer (depending on size), gently clip back a small amount of the top beak. Remember, you can always clip more if needed. Beaks have a "quick" and if you cut into it you will cause your hen pain. If you cut into the quick, apply Kwik Stop styptic powder (an anticoagulant you can get at the pet store) or cornstarch on your fingers and firmly position your fingers against the bleeding. Continue to apply pressure until the bleeding has subsided. Remember, chickens will peck at blood. Do not return the hen to the other birds until you know the bleeding has stopped.

If your hen's toenails get excessively long, use a dog or feline nail trimmer on the nails. Soak your hens feet in warm water for about five minutes to make this task easier. Cut back less than 1/3 of the nail. Fowl have a vein that runs down their toes and you don't want to cut into that. If you do, have some Kwik Stop handy and apply it right away.

Keeping Healthy Hens

Chickens can get sick and some of their ailments are serious and can wipe out an entire flock. Breathing difficulties, coughing/sneezing and watery discharge from their eyes or nose are signs that your hen is feeling foul. There is a lot you can do to keep your flock hale and hearty. Choose healthy, vaccinated birds and isolate new birds before introducing them to your flock. Keep their surroundings clean. Feed your flock a balanced diet. Don't overcrowd — overcrowding can cause illness. If you do have a sick or dead chicken — promptly remove it from the flock.

Any longtime chicken keeper will tell you, "No matter how clean you keep your area, your hens will eventually get bugs." Don't panic! The good news is the bugs that hang out on chickens can't tolerate the body temperature of a human — so if bugs get on you, they won't stay long. Zamzows' Mike Stanton recommends checking for mites and lice regularly. Local feed stores carry a livestock dust that is approved for poultry. Check the label and follow directions. Bear in mind, it's not enough to dust only the chickens. You will need to clean your chicken coop and dust it as well.

Chicken aficionado, Jim Schwartz of Parma, Idaho, uses old smudge pots in his coops to help ward off lice and mites. He uses

Smudge pot in coop. Jim Schwartz, Parma, Idaho.

them in a clever way. He and his wife Martha fill the pots with dry, airy dirt. On a regular basis they will add a little livestock dust. When their hens take a "dirt bath" the livestock dust is already mixed into the dirt — thus preventing the spread of lice and mites. "The old smudge pot is the perfect size for one hen," said Schwartz. "They can get in and out of it easily and the livestock dust is contained."

A dirt bath, is one of a chicken's favorite activities. It actually keeps them clean and free of bugs. If your ground is amenable to dust baths you might find wallows around your yard where your chickens are enjoying themselves.

An Ameraucana hen settles into a wallow and gives herself a dirt bath.

Rub-a-dub-dub! It is possible to water bathe a chicken. While it is not common practice to bathe your average backyard chicken, it is done often to show hens and roosters in competition. Mike Stanton says the birds actually "settle in" and enjoy the warm water. Incidentally, like any good pedicure, trimming a chicken's toe nails is made easier by a little pre-soak in some warm water first. *See Chapter 9 for directions on bathing your chicken.*

CHAPTER 9

4-H: You and Your Chicken

BY MAGGIE MINSHEW

With the increase in urban chicken keeping, 4-H organizations around the country have seen more and more children participating in 4-H poultry programs. City kids who never even thought about joining 4-H are now enjoying the benefits of being a part of a local club. A 4-H club is a group of five or more kids ages 5–18.

4-H has been around since 1902. According to 4-H.org, the National Institute of Food and Agriculture founded the 4-H Club. A gentleman by the name of A.B. Graham started 4-H in Clark County, Ohio. He called the first club "The Tomato Club" or the "Corn Growing Club." The organization evolved over the years and by 1912 they officially became 4-H clubs with the clover logo. Everyone asks, "What do the four Hs stand for?" Well, they stand for head, heart, hands, and health. The motto is, "To make the best BETTER!" In fact, many of your grandparents might remember in 1951, when the United States Postal Service honored 4-H with a 3-cent postage stamp.

1951 4-H postage stamp.

Today, 4-H isn't just about tomatoes, corn and farm animals. It is also about economics, engineering, and even rocket science. Kids also study sustainable energy, childhood obesity, and global food security. 4-H gives young people real life experience where they can learn and grow. In fact do you know what Reba McIntire, Dolly Parton and Orville Redenbacher all have in common? They, and many other celebrities spent time in 4-H.

Occasionally, you'll find schools that run the 4-H programs. However, most of the time, 4-H is managed by a local extension office, run by state universities or a county. There are more than 3,000 extension offices around the country. To find your local extension office, look in the phone book or search online.

One of the many opportunities 4-H has is the poultry program. The poultry program includes kids who raise pigeons, turkeys, ducks, geese and chickens. If you own an ostrich or even an emu, you would be welcome in 4-H. In and around Idaho's capital city, "the 4-H poultry project has seen steady growth over the last three years," said Brandi Kay, 4-H Program Coordinator for Ada County.

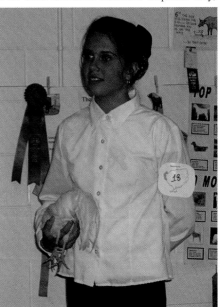
Lauren Hooker at a 4-H poultry show.

Susan Hooker of Boise, Idaho, was the leader for the "Birds of a Feather" 4-H club in Ada County. After 10 years of volunteering, she recently retired from the job. In the time she was a leader, the number of participants in her program tripled. "Most of my kids lived in town and kept their chickens in old dog runs or dog houses and they were definitely backyard chickens," said Hooker. She even offered a novice class for beginners in her program, which helped kids set and reach realistic goals. Hooker got involved with 4-H because her daughter had joined.

Here are highlights from Susan's program:

1) Her new members joined in October.
2) Participated in monthly meetings.
3) Learned about chicken keeping. These lessons included learning about the various types of hens: layers, fryers, and setters. They also learned about the many breeds of chickens. There are

more than 300 breeds! Kids also developed a good understanding of the different diseases that can harm chickens, and became very familiar with chicken anatomy and biology.

4) In February and March, club members would order their chicks. The kids had to order them early so that the chickens would be old enough to show in late summer.

5) Between the time they ordered the chicks and received them, participants would learn how to properly handle the birds.

6) They learned how to wash the birds and trim their toenails to have them ready to show. (*See instructions on the following page.*)

7) Kids learned how to clip their wings, how to check for a pasty vent, and they also learned important aspects of chicken feed.

8) Prior to taking the birds to the fair, they would participate in 4-H Fun Days where the kids would learn about showing poultry through test runs.

9) Then the big day would come when they go to the fair. They are tested on knowledge, handling, cleanliness, and journal keeping, among many things.

Tips for successful poultry showing in 4-H:

Tip #1: Pick the right chicken for your 4-H poultry project. My advice is to stay away from Lakenvelder and Leghorn chickens because they are "flighty" and hard to handle. Most leaders recommend banty chickens because they are smaller and easier to handle with smaller hands.

Tip #2: Sit with your chicken and have it on a carpet square so the chicken will become used to being handled by you. Do this a lot.

Tip #3: Know that the second most important thing about your chicken feed is the protein content. So ... the most important thing about your feed is knowing the manufacture date. You don't want to feed your chickens out-of-date feed.

It wasn't all about showmanship at the fair. Part of being in 4-H is doing volunteer work. Hooker says she and the children would do various volunteer events, including going to nursing homes at Christmas and Easter time and showing their chickens. The residents said that it was the cherry on top of their day!

So if you're interested in getting yourself and your backyard chicken involved with 4-H, be sure to contact your local extension office and enroll before October.

Mike Stanton's Chicken Washing Formula

This method of preparing birds for a show is a combination of techniques some of our bird club members use. This method is what is known as the dunk method. You will need: four tubs (deep enough for water to cover the chickens body, but not its head), baking soda, soap (a mild dish soap or shampoo is best), fabric softener (not the concentrated type), glycerin for colored birds and bluing for white birds. To bathe your bird, "dunk" their bodies in each tub. Have your hen spend enough time in each tub to allow her to get clean and fully benefit from the mixtures.

First soak the bird's feet for a few minutes, then clip the bird's nails and beak. File both with a nail file to make them look natural. (*See page 63 for additional information on nail and beak trimming.*) While the bird is in the water, use a soft brush (a baby hairbrush works well) to loosen the muck on the birds feathers. A soft bristle toothbrush can be used to clean the comb, face and wattles. Remember to plug the bird's nostrils before dunking/rinsing!

Use a medium toothbrush to remove dirt from the legs and toes. Clean up under the scales on the legs and toes, scrubbing against the scale.

Tub #1

To warm water (not hot water) add: a heaping tablespoon of baking soda, soap (start with a teaspoon), just until the water feels slick between your fingers and 1/8 cup fabric softener.

Tub #2

Mix warm water with a heaping tablespoon of baking soda and 1/8 cup fabric softener.

MAKE SURE ALL SOAP IS RINSED FROM THE FEATHERS

Tub #3

Mix warm water with a heaping tablespoon of baking soda. If bathing white birds, add 2 drops of bluing (work bluing into the water well, blue splotches on the birds is a disqualification). If bathing colored birds skip the bluing and add 3 drops of glycerin, mix well.

Tub #4

Mix warm water with a heaping tablespoon of baking soda and 1/8 cup fabric softener (this is the same as tub #2), with the additions of 2 or 3 drops of glycerin if bathing colored birds, none if bathing a white bird.

Gently towel dry your bird. You may need several towels. Do not put your bird outside in cold weather after you have bathed it. After the bird is bathed, it is very important to keep it housed in a clean cage. Keep the bird on dry shavings or straw until it is completely dry. Dust and dirt sticks to wet feathers.

If you have white birds use baby power around the vent area if it remains stained after the bath.

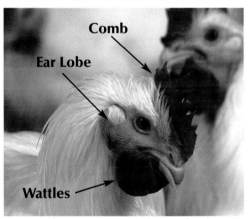

Comb

Ear Lobe

Wattles

With proper care, your chickens' comb and wattles will shine.

A solution of equal parts alcohol and glycerin lightly rubbed into the comb and wattles with a cotton swab will make the red stand out. This can be done the night before judging or if time allows in the morning before judging. Put a light coat of baby oil on the feet at the time of coop-in (keeps the droppings off the feet). Be careful not to get any of the oil on the feathers.

NOTE ON USING BLUING: Know your bird's feather quality, soft or hard. A soft feathered bird (such as Silkies, Cochins, etc.) will take the bluing more readily, so you may want to skip the bluing entirely or use only 1/2 to 1 drop of bluing.

NOTE: Birds should be given their bath 3–5 days before they are to be judged or entered in a show. This allows the bird to preen and condition the feathers into perfect position and condition.

CHAPTER 10

The Backyard Chicken Fight: Making Headlines

Ask anyone who has backyard chickens and they will tell you, they are more than "just chickens." They are producers, performers and pets, and in many cases, members of the family. Unlike dogs or cats they rarely are seen lounging or sleeping through the day. They are always busy. They are non-stop foragers, curious about almost everything and fertilize whatever is in their path. Chickens will rid a backyard of bugs, slugs and weeds. They also provide you with a bounty of nutritious, organic, fresh eggs. It's been said that if your life is filled with meaning and purpose you live a happier life. From experience, I can tell you that just four or five little hens will give you purpose. They give you a reason to put both feet on the floor each morning and venture out to make certain all is well in their simple world.

USDA poster promoting chicken keeping.

During World War I, the U.S. Department of Agriculture promoted the notion of everyone keeping chickens in their backyard as a patriotic duty. One could argue that the current backyard chicken movement is an attempt to return to a simpler time — much like life was in the early part of the 20th century. In 2004, Madison, Wisconsin, was among the first of a number of cities to change laws allowing restricted numbers of chickens.

New York City has long allowed chickens. The birds live in urban areas in Chicago, Portland, Seattle and other big cities. A 2008 Newsweek Magazine article reported that 65% of America's largest cities allow the keeping of chickens. As the urban chicken movement has gained momentum in the past few years, surely that number is higher. For the most part, crowing roosters maintain an outlaw status, and backyard chickens cannot be butchered and processed for meat in most communities. Though the U.S. Department of Agriculture doesn't keep statistics on small-scale chicken tending, anecdotally, there is a growing number of people committed to living a more sustainable life and raising chickens in suburban and urban areas. Most people are keeping the birds for eggs, not meat.

Try to tell the owners of small backyard flocks they aren't allowed to keep the chickens, and you'll likely end up with a fight on your hands. Backyard chickens tend to live the good life as "pets" — whether it's free ranging around a swing set in California or part of a rooftop garden in New York. There are many reasons why this "backyard chicken movement" is sweeping the nation — and in other countries as well. Perhaps it's part and parcel of the fervent eco-movement across the country, like urban gardens, recycling programs and reducing one's carbon footprint.

The following are brief "chicken fight" stories and a few interesting anecdotes from around the United States. These are stories of Americans, many with a secret stash of hens in their backyard, who believe you *can* fight City Hall. While many small towns and municipalities have waged their own fights, these are the ones that made headlines. The desire for locally grown food, and freedom from food treated with unwanted hormones or chemicals, is motivating many city folk to not only plant large, bountiful gardens, but to raise their own chickens for eggs. The determination of the chicken keepers is inspiring.

The one fight that perhaps garnered the most national attention was in Oregon's capital, Salem.

OREGON

"You could keep a 100-pound potbellied pig in your yard, but not a three pound chicken," recalls Barbara Palermo, leader of Salem's Chickens In The Yard (CITY). In the autumn of 2010, the fine chicken-keeping folks of Salem, Oregon, won a huge victory as the city council finally approved an ordinance that allows people to keep three backyard chickens (no roosters) within the city limits. The fight lasted nearly 24-months with the zoning issue going before the council more than 10 times. In that time, their fight made the front page of the prestigious Wall Street Journal [July '09].

Now, chicken owners must pay an annual $50 licensing fee, coops cannot be any larger than 10x12 feet and must be 20-feet away from a neighboring lot. "We worked hard for two years trying to get our elected representatives to adopt a chicken-keeping policy," said Barbara Palermo. "I even produced a movie *"The Chicken Revolution"* about our efforts, which won an award in a local film festival. In that movie we make fun of opponents who suggested chicken coops would lead to meth labs. Sometimes it takes a lot of publicity that embarrasses the city to get their

Barbara Palermo with Florence and Shaniqua.

attention and make changes," said Palermo. She was frustrated because at the time she was asking to keep four small chickens in her backyard, the city allowed potbellied pigs. "It was also a property rights issue," added Palermo. "And, we pay a lot of property taxes in Oregon."

Additional to the licensing fee, chicken keepers must agree to, and pay for, an inspection every three years. Palermo calls Salem's ordinance one of the most restrictive in the country. She and CITY are hoping it can be modified in the coming months.

At the same time, Salem's neighbor to the north, Beaverton, was working toward a backyard chicken agreement. "It actually went very smoothly," said supporter Julia Sathler, of Beaverton. "It really wasn't a 'chicken fight' so-to-speak, we just had to be very patient." In the fall of 2010 the Beaverton City Council gave the thumbs up to keeping chickens. Sathler doesn't have her own backyard flock but passionately supports food security and eating locally. She helped shepherd the change in the ordinance which took the better part of a year. Business owner, Mark Ludeman, was selling chicks out of his home store (by the same name, Ludemans) in Beaverton at the time Sathler and friends were trying to get a favorable ordinance. Ludeman helped with the cause. "Beaverton is pro-business and I think the council wanted to support Ludemans," added Sathler.

At the final council meeting, when the ordinance passed, Mark Ludeman and Sathler said they weren't sure what happened — because it happened so quickly without much discussion. "They voted, it passed and I'll be selling chicks in the spring," said Ludeman.

Beaverton now allows four hens per residence; the coop must be at least 20-feet from a neighbor's home and no front yard chickens. In other Oregon communities, the Gresham City Council legalized chicken keeping in December 2010 where you can have unlimited "livestock," provided they are kept 100-feet from neighbors, which is possible only on uncommonly large lots. Springfield allows residents up to four hens, in Eugene, the limit is two.

CALIFORNIA

Currently there are nearly 50 cities or counties in California that have adopted some sort of chicken keeping ordinance. There have been numerous fights throughout the state with several being quite vocal. Cities that neighbor Nevada, such as Grass Valley and Nevada City, are in the midst of a backyard chicken ordinance debate. Pro-chicken keepers in Truckee lobbied their local government as well. Truckee adopted a chicken keeping ordinance in November 2010 and now residents can keep hens. The number of hens depends on the lot size — starting at two hens per 2,500 square feet.

In Sacramento, the Campaign to Legalize Urban Chicken Keeping (CLUCK), has spent nearly two years trying to get a pro chicken law approved. "Timing was a huge issue and did not work in our favor," said Abi Crouch of CLUCK. "Our issue was gaining momentum just as the elections occurred. We lost the momentum and now we have new council members and we have to start all over again." With the Sacramento proposed chicken ordinance in limbo, Crouch estimates there are hundreds of people keeping chickens on the sly. "We try to stay under the radar," adds Crouch who has a small backyard flock. "The law states 'no livestock including poultry.'" Ironically, pro-poultry Fair Oaks is located just 10-miles up the road. Their city mascot is a chicken.

Throughout California there are flocks of feral (undomesticated) chickens. They ostensively live off the land, reproduce and continue to do so — which has been a problem in some California communities. About an hour north of Sacramento in Sonoma County, residents can keep up to six chickens. That's because of a plucky little lady who wouldn't take no for an answer. Doreen Proctor started caring for feral chickens in 1997. "They would just come into our yard after our old dogs passed away," recounts Proctor. She put out food and they would lay eggs in the nests she made for them. All was well until a

Doreen Proctor and Bertah.

neighbor reported her to the county in 2007. "I had 30 days to get rid of all my pet chickens after receiving that 'courtesy notice' from Sonoma County. They [the hens] don't smell and they're hardly ever noisy unless they lay an egg or see a hawk," added the 77-year-old retired health professional. Proctor refused to give up her hens so she asked for an extension (actually, many over a two-year period), and the county granted the extensions. That gave her enough time to get other neighbors to sign a petition and have friends mount a letter-writing campaign to the county. "I was devastated, I had to do something. A lot of people move here because of the country atmosphere." Proctor even had a little help from a friendly editor at the Sonoma Index Tribune.

Sonoma County passed an amendment in December of 2009. Residents can keep up to six hens in their backyard. Proctor, who is a Master Gardner, says she tries to keep just six, but often people drop off chicks and hens to her as if she were a safe house for poultry. She still has one of her original feral chickens. "Tac" is more than 13-years-old and Proctor believes she is a Speckled Sussex. Tac's sisters, Tic and Toe, have gone to the big chicken coop in the sky. Even at 13, Tac is still able to fly onto Proctor's deck, then to the roof of the house and continue into a big oak tree in the front yard. She has watched Tac and other mamma hens fend off hawks when they have baby chicks. "The feral chickens are tough but can become friendly. They don't like to be picked up though," cautions Proctor.

The chicken keeping trend has grown so much that in Santa Clarita, California, residents there were recently surveyed on their opinions regarding urban chickens. My friend, Barbara C. Morris received this form in the mail and found it very interesting that the USDA was querying her.

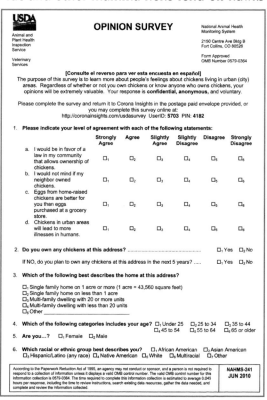

2010 USDA survey on chicken keeping.

Barbara hasn't received follow up from the USDA and where she lives there are no specific policies prohibiting chickens. "Keeping chickens in ones patio might violate some of our other rules that apply to nuisance or noise. We're a townhome community and the units just have small patios," said Barbara.

COLORADO

Denver has long allowed backyard chickens but soon the city may ask voters to decide whether to permit poultry pets without prior approval. Currently, Denverites must go through an arduous process that includes notifying their next door neighbors, paying a $150 fee ($50 annually after the first year), getting authorization from a city zoning administrator and approval from the city's animal care and control. "It's a lengthy and difficult process," said Sundari Kraft of Denver's EatWhereULive and author of The Complete Idiot's Guide to Urban Homesteading. "Neighbors can easily block the process and you have to place a zoning sign in your yard."

Sundari Kraft and Cardamom.

Kraft, who supports urban sustainability and doesn't want a public vote on the matter, keeps hens and goats. "We get healthy eggs from our hens and all the milk we can drink from our two Nigerian Dwarf Goats." Kraft is part of a city appointed Sustainable Food Policy Council. The council will make a recommendation to Denver Mayor John W. Hickenlooper. The group is in the process of developing a carefully crafted "Food-Producing Animals" ordinance. "We want the ordinance to include reasonable guidelines with adequate oversight," said Kraft. "We will also be very organized when we present our proposal to the mayor and council." Kraft cautions others that going into a hearing unprepared would be foolish. "You need to know how everyone will vote, or you're wasting your time." That's where a lot of preparation and lobbying is needed prior to bringing an ordinance to a council. Kraft says their group will identify specific issues that each council member might have and address those prior to the hearing. She is hoping the council will approve a request for residents to keep eight fowl — a mix of various poultry.

North of Denver, in Greeley, the fight to legally keep chickens was very much in the forefront. Neighboring Durango, Fort Collins, and Longmont, all allow chickens but in Greeley it's not that clearcut. There was confusion as to whether keeping chickens fell under the livestock or pet ordinances. "We want to get to where we are a little more sustainable," said Cassie Kauffman, who along with her husband Britton, are Greeley natives. They kept an online journal of their fight to legally keep chickens in their backyard after they were cited by the city for raising their flock. They live within the city limits — but right on the boundary line. Neighbors across the street freely keep poultry. The proposal would have allowed up to six backyard hens, as long as sanitation, predator-proofing and distance from neighbors conditions were met.

Britton and Cassie Kauffman with Omelette in the background.

During the final hearing on the proposal, the city council chamber was filled. There was public comment both for and against keeping backyard chickens. Those who testified against the proposed clarification were worried about noise, smell and humane care of the birds. "All they do is poop on stuff and wake us up early in the morning with their stupid chirping, and then they flitter around spreading feathers," said one bird opponent. "The only good bird is Extra Crispy Kentucky Fried Chicken." Even an advisory committee of 15 interested citizens couldn't sway the council. During the public comment period, one woman testified how her drug dealing friend kept his drugs hidden inside his chicken coop. "We all rolled our eyes and thought, what next?" said Britton Kauffman. Shortly after that, an account of the public comment and an illustration of a roasted chicken appeared on Kauffman's website: www.lifetransplanet.com. "The issue

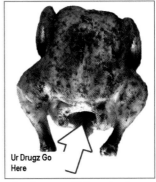

Ur Drugz Go Here

Courtesy: www.lifetransplanet.com

ended in a tie vote with the mayor absent and unable to break the tie," added the Kauffmans. Ironically, Mayor Tom Norton was not in attendance during the meeting due to an economic development trip. He was touting Greeley and northern Colorado as a terrific place for Pilgrim's Pride to set up shop. Pilgrim's Pride is the largest commercial chicken producer in the United States. "As it turns out, the law is still vague, but we get to keep our chickens under the domesticated bird code," said the Kauffmans.

FLORIDA

In the Sunshine State, not all is sunny for those who want to keep chickens. While St. Augustine and Jacksonville are two places you may have a little backyard flock, there are other cities like St. Augustine Beach and Sarasota, where you can't. Sarasota resident Jono Miller wants to move toward a more sustainable way of life. His group, Sarasota CLUCK (Citizens Lobbying for Urban Chicken Keeping), was disheartened by the reception from the Sarasota Planning Board. The backyard chicken proposal was shot down in late 2010 by a 2–3 vote. Sarasota CLUCK will take the issue to the City Commission. "We will be very organized when we attend that meeting," said Miller. "We have organized our group to meet with neighborhood associations to make certain the groups are informed. We're also looking at bringing in non-typical chicken keepers to testify." Sarasota is a hip community and Miller wants to demonstrate that young, upwardly mobile professionals desire to keep chickens and live a more sustainable life. They are hoping for a code that would give Sarasotans the right to keep four chickens per backyard without regulations or enforcement. "Those people who think chickens are obnoxious, noisy and smelly keep asking about enforcement," added Miller. "We think if Seattle can allow eight chickens per yard, we should be okay with four, without enforcement."

About 260 miles northeast of Sarasota, the Floridians of St. Augustine Beach are fighting the good fight as well. Non-chicken owners, Dave and Nana Royer, are leading the cause to be chicken owners. Before getting her little flock, Nana thought it best to ask permission rather than beg forgiveness. "St. Augustine proper allows chickens, as long as they're contained on a lot. St Augustine Beach, where I live however, does not." said Royer. St. Augustine Beach is just 2.5 square miles and located just across the Intracoastal Waterway from several colleges. "Opponents argued that if we allow chickens then people will want goats and pigs. They also said the chickens will cause foul

Dave and Nana Royer in their chickenless yard.

odors, spread disease, and they claimed college kids would get chickens and not properly care for them." Royer went before the city commissioners, but her anti-chicken neighbor also brought in support. "I got all my neighbors to sign a petition in favor of me having a few hens, and my one anti-chicken neighbor, drafted his own petition against the proposal and compelled the same neighbors to sign it!" The commission chose to not vote on the proposal at that time — which Royer says is actually good. She believes it would have been voted down. When Royer goes back to the St.

Augustine Beach City Commissioners, she says she'll be more organized. She'll ask a health professional to testify on her behalf that chickens can be kept in clean surroundings, they don't harbor disease and coop smells are minimal if properly maintained. She'll also bring in more supporters and offer testimony that shows other communities successfully implementing chicken keeping codes.

GEORGIA

Since 2005 folks in Atlanta have legally kept backyard chickens. Other smaller communities near Atlanta, such as Duluth and Athens, have approved them as well. However, the city of Winder is currently wrestling with the idea. Commissioners would have to change the current livestock ordinance. The subject of backyard chickens was an occasional topic during the 2010 candidate forums. It is likely to be a topic of consideration with the new 2011 commissioners.

IDAHO

In my home state of Idaho, there haven't been any major chicken fights. Our capital city, Boise, allows up to three "pet" hens per residence. The North End of Boise is highly populated with happy poultry. Neighboring Nampa also allows three chickens per yard. Both cities have nixed roosters.

ILLINOIS

In Evanston, Illinois, there was a 36-year ban on raising chickens if you lived within the city limits. That's all changed. In September of 2010 the Evanston City Council voted to allow backyard chickens by a 6–3 vote. It took one year and 75 people who belonged to the group Evanston Backyard Chickens, to lobby the city. The group's patience and hard work paid off. "I think this is a small step for chickens and a big step for sustainability and green life in Evanston," said Aharon Solomon, a member of Evanston Backyard Chickens. The group set up a website and created an online petition in favor of keeping hens. Those who were keeping chickens prior to the approval would offer curious, would-be hen keepers, secret backyard chicken coop tours. "It was all in an effort to educate the public in a small grass roots kind of way," one supporter said.

Now, there are guidelines within the newly passed ordinance for proper coop construction and maintenance. Chicken keepers must notify their neighbors before receiving a license, but they don't need a neighbor's approval before obtaining hens. There is a $50 licensing fee. Evanston has also limited the coop licenses. Only 20 will be issued in the first year.

The outcome for the residents in Lombard, Illinois, was not as favorable for those wanting to keep chickens. In December of 2010 the proposal was shot down after the Village Board heard testimony from those concerned with the health and environmental issues. The Lombard Board of Trustees voted 5–1 against the request to allow chickens in residential areas of Lombard Village. "We are taking this as a setback, not a defeat, and are working to build more support for local foods systems and backyard chickens before making another push for change," said Emily Prasad, founder of Citizens of Lombard for Urban Chickens (CLUC). "We were very frustrated by how difficult it was to get the trustees to take this as a serious issue. They seemed to be either unwilling or unable to be educated on the subject. Despite our evidence, they choose to be swayed by residents claiming all the usual grievances: noise, sanitation, property values decreasing, increased pests/predators." CLUC said the board voted against the measure with virtually no additional discussion. The group, like so many others around the country, advocates the production of fresh, local eggs as a sustainable food source. They are currently making plans to develop a more robust local foods system, in the hopes that education will pave the way toward more acceptance of backyard chickens.

IOWA

The Cedar Rapids Citizens for the Legalization of Urban Chickens (CR-CLUC), pecked away at their city hall for six months. In August of 2010 the Cedar Rapids council approved an ordinance to allow residents to keep up to six hens on their residential property. Each backyard flock must be fenced, 10-feet from any property line and 25-feet from neighboring homes. And, no stinky

Mary, RD Benion and Comet at Christmas time.

chickens are allowed. "Odors from the manure can't be 'perceptible' beyond the boundaries of the yard," reads the ordinance. It is a one year trial period, there is a $25 fee and you must band (leg identification) the birds.

In the small town of Palo, Iowa, (population about 900), the city council unanimously approved the keeping of backyard chickens. "It was a fairly quick process with just three readings," said Mary Benion, Palo resident and USPS letter carrier. "There was one person opposed to the proposal — but we prevailed." Benion went to the meetings with a petition signed by 25 supporters including her neighbors. The Cedar Rapids chicken fight was what sparked Mary's interest. "I had been following what was happening in Cedar Rapids and after my husband, RD, and I lost our dog to old age, we debated whether to get another dog or chickens. We opted for poultry," added Benion. They constructed a nice looking portable chicken tractor coop with an attached run for their four hens. Now, they are happily collecting eggs and letting their brood entertain them.

MASSACHUSETTS

The cities of Amherst, Arlington and Springfield found themselves mired in backyard chicken fights in the latter part of the decade. But, in Weston, Massachusetts, there is an innovative program that encourages backyard chicken keeping with a program that allows would-be hen keepers to "try before they buy." In this New England town, there is a non-profit organization, Land's Sake Farm, that offers prospective chicken keepers a "Rent-a-Coop" with everything inside. For $150 (including a refundable $50 deposit) customers get a two-week rental of one chicken tractor coop, two chickens (Light Brahmas for

Land's Sake Rent-a-Coop.

their docile nature), organic feed, bedding, water and feed trays, and instructions for chicken care. Plus, further instruction is just a phone call away. Land's Sake Farm delivers the chickens and everything you need to keep them. At the end of the 14-day trial period, Land's Sake returns to reclaim the coop and its contents.

Land's Sake doesn't sell the chickens and coop setup, it's strictly a rental program. "We've seen some pretty teary farewells," said Douglas Cook, Education Director at Land's Sake. "That's why it's fairly common for customers to extend the rental period." Cook says it works well for a lot of people who don't necessarily want to "winter" chickens. The program has been such a success that Land's Sake usually has a waiting list.

The community of Belmont, Massachusetts, likes their chickens so much that they held a benefit for the new local library with a coop tour.

The "All Cooped Up" tour had residents visiting nine Belmont hen houses. Admission cost $5–$20 with each participant receiving a map to the fanciful and inventive coops. Linda Atkinson, a

The "All Cooped Up" tour, Adine Storer, Belmont, Massachusetts.

Belmont Library Foundation member and organizer of the coop tour, has been keeping up to five hens for more than three years. The popular tour of eight backyards included the home/coop owners who welcomed participants into their yards and answered questions from all the curious attendees.

MICHIGAN

If there is one state that is conflicted over backyard chickens, it's Michigan. From city to city there is a love/hate relationship with poultry. In Ann Arbor, East Lansing and Traverse City, laying hens are welcome. But in Detroit, Flint and Grand Rapids, it's the opposite. They don't want chickens in the city. Grand Rapids officials recently warned underground chicken owners that if there is a chicken complaint, the city will investigate and enforce the ban on hens in the backyard.

Rick and Brenda Beerhorst have kept chickens for more than three years. A complaint was filed against them and that's when the issue ended up on the steps of City Hall. "It literally galvanized the people here in Grand Rapids," said Rick Beerhorst. There were several hearings where people testified for and against a proposed ordinance that would have allowed chicken keeping. During one of the last hearings, the council chambers were packed and everyone seemed moved

Beerhorst children holding their hens.

by one young person who offered her opinion. "This 12-year-old girl got up and testified," recounts Beerhorst. "Though she was only 12, she was so eloquent with what she was reading. It turns out that she had discovered the United States Department of Agriculture's 1917 poster (the poster at the beginning of these stories) that encourages all Americans to 'keep hens and raise chickens.'" The proposed ordinance in Grand Rapids would have allowed residents to keep up to five hens in their yard.

The proposal failed by one vote. However, the good people of Grand Rapids haven't given up. "One city council member said if the group could gather 1,000 signatures in favor of keeping hens, he would change his vote," added Beerhorst.

There are other Michigan cities on the threshold of allowing chickens; Burton, Cadillac and Petoskey.

MINNESOTA

In Minneapolis, the law is fairly lenient. Residents can keep an unlimited number of chickens but must have consent from 80% of neighbors within 100-feet of property lines and chickens must be confined with proper shelter.

To serve the many homeless birds, a one-of-a-kind organization emerged in 2001. Chicken Run Rescue (CRR) fosters critical thought about "who is food and who is friend" through rescue, rehabilitation, adoption and education. CRR rescues domestic fowl impounded by the Minneapolis Animal Care and Control and the Humane Society, who come their way as a result of abandonment, abuse or neglect.

CRR's adoption terms:
- Love them for who they are not for what can be taken from them.
- Keep the bird for life (chickens can live up to 14 years).
- Prohibit slaughter, breeding, fighting or exhibit.
- Limit adoption as a companion animal only — not a food animal. Use of eggs OK for personal consumption, not OK to sell, barter or hatch.

Mary Britton Clouse,
founder Chicken Run Rescue.

- Provide proper care including food, water and shelter.
- Provide fresh air and exercise, companionship (with other same species animals) and veterinary care as for any other companion animal.
- Adoptions are limited to within 90 miles of the Minneapolis/St. Paul vicinity.

CRR says there is an increasing interest in adopting chickens as companions, but the number of incoming birds has increased by more than 500% since 2009. Their motto: Don't breed or buy, adopt! "There are never enough homes for displaced animals," says Mary Britton Clouse, founder of Chicken Run Rescue.

Minneapolis' neighbor, Bloomington, approved a hen keeping ordinance in November of 2010. However, only 20% of the city's population is able to keep hens due to the stipulation that chicken coops must be at least 50-feet from residential property lines. Still, 80% of yards in Minneapolis can't accommodate that restriction.

OHIO

The swanky community of Bexley, Ohio, joined the likes of Cleveland, Columbus and Toledo in December of 2010 by approving a set of revised pet ordinances. The rules are similar to other pro-chicken communities where there are:

- No roosters
- No selling eggs
- Must get free permit within 60 days of procuring chickens
- Chickens must be kept in a coop in the backyard

It's likely the Bexley hens will have pretty nice accommodations. One area of the East Side suburb is reportedly ranked among the top 100 richest neighborhoods in the U.S., with a median family income of more than $300,000.

Bexley is chirping over chicks.

UTAH

All along Utah's Wasatch Front, communities have approved backyard chicken keeping. The city of Layton passed a law in February of 2010. The city council there wrestled with the chicken issue for months. Some council members were worried that by passing a chicken-friendly ordinance, it would open doors to people wanting permission to keep bees and pigeons. So far, that hasn't happened. Along with Layton, Pleasant Grove, West Jordan and West Valley City all adopted hen keeping ordinances. Even big Salt Lake City approved an ordinance in late spring of 2010.

However, all the Utah communities saying "yes" to chickens haven't swayed the Ogden Planning Commission or the Ogden City Council. The commission and the council have considered a proposal to keep backyard chickens several times. The most recent rejection came in October of 2010. The planning commission feared that residents who didn't take proper care of chickens could have an adverse impact on neighbors. Additionally, the commission reported the city's Code Enforcement Department did not have adequate funds to enforce a chicken ordinance.

Mayor Matthew Godfrey advised the city council to reject the proposed ordinance because he believed it would be difficult to enforce licensing. He added, "The ordinance could also cause the chicken population to become unmanageable because of the city's burgeoning Hispanic population. The Hispanic culture is used to having chickens." These comments infuriated the people who attended the meeting and Godfrey was the target of some tough criticism in online postings for days after the council gathering. "How did we get so far from what is so natural and good for people?" said former Ogden City Council candidate, Dave Wolfgram. He, his wife Shauna, and others worked hard to

Wolfgram's youngest son, Kaleb, after discovering their flock's first egg.

educate the city and residents about the urban chicken movement through workshops and meetings they organized during local farmers markets and on Facebook. "In Ogden you can own 100 pigeons but not a couple of laying hens," added Wolfgram. "We're going back in the spring with another proposed ordinance change."

Wolfgram's Campine hen, helping herself to the garden.

Just about 90 minutes southeast of Ogden you'll find an annual arts festival that has been known to include "Chicken Poop Bingo" as part of its annual offerings. It involves one giant sized bingo card and one chicken. Just as you may well imagine, you pick a number, pay your money … and wait.

VIRGINIA

Near our country's capital, there is an ongoing backyard chicken fight. Would-be chicken keepers in Prince William County (northern Virginia) have gone before the Board of County Supervisors, but the issue was sent back to the Planning Commission. In November 2010 the Commission ruled in favor of residents who live on agriculturally zoned property, on one or more acres, or live in Prince William County's Rural Crescent area. Manassas' Vic Cole, who is a chicken proponent, says there is more to do. "It's a victory if you live on designated ag land. But as it's written, I can't keep hens where I live," said Cole, who prefers fresh eggs and is partial to Golden Buffs (Sex Link hens).

The retired Navy commander pointed out flaws in the county code that might help his cause. "A resident here can keep horses on two or more acres, but the way the code is written they can't keep chickens." Cole said it was so egregious that everyone agreed. "I kept asking someone to explain why this was and no one could answer me." Cole is continuing his crusade to win approval and now has the Farm Bureau behind the cause. "The Farm Bureau has sent a recommendation to the county that it approve backyard chickens."

WASHINGTON

Seattle, Tacoma, and in late 2010, Bremerton, approved backyard chickens. These large cities either re-worked current code or adopted new ones to encourage more urban farming. Their neighbor Federal Way, was still debating loosening a fairly restrictive code as late as November of 2010. "The new ordinance will allow any combination of four chickens and/or ducks on residential lots less than 35,000 square feet," said Matt Herrera, Federal Way chicken advocate. On lots 35,000 square feet and larger, a maximum of 20 chickens/ducks will be allowed. Roosters are banned except for areas zoned "suburban estates." Such areas are zoned low density with five acre minimum lot sizes, which also allow animal husbandry as a primary use. "The council modified the staff and Planning Commission recommendation to include three acceptable coop designs with the ability to request a modification if a different coop of equal or superior design is used," added Herrera. The new ordinance will take effect in early 2011.

WISCONSIN

While the final state in this catalog of The Backyard Chicken Fight is Wisconsin, it was actually one of the first states to witness the fight to legally keep backyard hens. One could argue Madison, Wisconsin, actually started it all. There was a grassroots movement to legalize chicken keeping in 2004. The code was successfully changed, allowing chicken keeping on single-family home properties. In Madison you can have up to four hens, and the coops must be no closer than 25-feet from the nearest neighbor's yard. Folks in Madison have been

happily keeping chickens in their backyards ever since. In fact, a well-known feature length documentary "Mad City Chickens," came out of the Madison experience in 2009. The filmmakers use humor, anecdotes and facts to tell their story and further the cause of urban chicken farming.

Despite Madison being the trendsetter, other Wisconsin communities have been slow to follow. Caledonia, Fond du Lac and Maryville all specifically say "no thanks" to the humble backyard chicken.

One added bit of interest, none of the states currently fighting over chickens has poultry as its state bird. However, Delaware with its Blue Hen and Rhode Island with its Rhode Island Red both claim the unassuming chicken as their state bird.

* * *

As more and more people desire small-scale chicken farming, the trend toward keeping backyard chickens will continue to grow. But, likely not before there is a fight in many more communities — reminding us of an old Henry Ford saying, "Business is never so healthy as when, like a chicken, it must do a certain amount of scratching around for what it gets." Here's to the men and women who scratch around for what they get!

Gretchen Anderson

Overly curious by nature, Gretchen Anderson is an award-winning, humor columnist, author and former television news anchor/reporter. Her news stories have been carried on NBC, ABC and CNN around the globe. Gretchen has been published in various magazines and newspapers and in 2010 collaborated on a book of poetry. You can read her humor columns at www.theindnews.com. Her five children and one great husband keep her going six different directions.

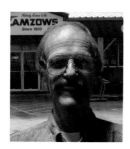

Mike Stanton

In many circles, Mike Stanton is referred to as "The Chicken Man." Stanton is currently the assistant manager at Zamzows in Nampa, Idaho. As the former Idaho representative to the American Poultry Association he has raised chickens for more than 40 years. He also served as president of the Idaho Bird Breeders Association. Stanton specializes in bird breeding practices that maintain clean genetic pools. He has helped breed endangered pheasants from China and Vietnam. The life-long chickener lives on a farm in Weiser, Idaho, with his wife Becky, her many cats, and countless chickens.

Maggie Minshew

Always up for a new challenge, Maggie took to caring for chickens very easily. From an early age, this mature 5th grader has had a flare for writing. Maggie has spent numerous hours observing her backyard chickens and their behaviors. She is a trusted pet owner of four hens, two dogs, one hamster and a 5-year-old fair fish.

References and other places for good information on backyard chickens:

- 4-h.org
- backyardchickens.com/forum
- brittonclouse.com/chickenrunrescue
- chicken-revolution.com
- elaineambrose.com
- facebook.com/pages/The-Backyard-Chicken-Fight/126457854071940
- forthebirdscc.com
- hensaver.com
- home.centurytel.net/thecitychicken
- lifetransplanet.com
- msnyderarch.com
- tarazod.com
- zamzows.com